LIZARDS IN CAPTIVITY
PS-769

The **College** of West Anglia

FRONT ENDPAPERS: *Eublepharis macularius.* BACK END-
PAPERS: *Heloderma suspectum.* Photos by Ken Lucas, Steinhart
Aquarium.

To the folks and Susie.

ISBN 0-87666-921-6

Distributed in the U.S. by T.F.H. Publications, Inc., 211 West Sylvania
Avenue, PO Box 427, Neptune, NJ 07753; in England by T.F.H. (Gt. Britain)
Ltd., 13 Nutley Lane, Reigate, Surrey; in Canada to the pet trade by Rolf C.
Hagen Ltd., 3225 Sartelon Street, Montreal 382, Quebec; in Canada to the
book trade by H & L Pet Supplies, Inc., 27 Kingston Crescent, Kitchener,
Ontario N28 2T6; in Southeast Asia by Y.W. Ong, 9 Lorong 36 Geylang,
Singapore 14; in Australia and the South Pacific by Pet Imports Pty. Ltd.,
P.O. Box 149, Brookvale 2100, N.S.W. Australia; in South Africa by Valid
Agencies, P.O. Box 51901, Randburg 2125 South Africa. Published by T.F.H.
Publications, Inc., Ltd., the British Crown Colony of Hong Kong.

639.39T Z W 0608604(ω)639.3950

LIZARDS
IN CAPTIVITY

RICHARD H. WYNNE

The red tegu, *Tupinambis rufescens* (Teiidae). Photo by H. Hansen, Aquarium Berlin.

A racerunner, *Cnemidophorus lemniscatus* (Teiidae). Photo by K. Lucas, Steinhart Aquarium.

The caiman lizard, *Dracaena guianensis* (Teiidae). Photo by H. Hansen, Aquarium Berlin.

The eyed lizard, *Lacerta lepida* (Lacertidae). Photo by H. Hansen, Aquarium Berlin.

ACKNOWLEDGMENTS

I would like to express my thanks to the following people who have contributed to this project over the years: Mr. and Mrs. R. A. Wynne; David Childers; Steve Crane; Kathryn Shanks; Toni Brannon Crane; Janice Prather; David Barker; Jim Murphy; Ardell Mitchell; Charles Carpenter; John Reba; Susan Campbell; Bill Lamareaux; Ray Guese; Mike Stower; Henry Aschner; Andy Johnson; Wayne Seifert; Chris Seifert; Jim Brockett; Barney Tomberlin; Jim Dunlap; and Robert Klein.

Lacerta lilfordi. G. Marcuse photo.

Contents

The green lizard, *Lacerta viridis* (Lacertidae). Photo by H. Hansen, Aquarium Berlin.

The common iguana, *Iguana iguana* (Iguanidae). Photo by J. Dommers. Note the greatly enlarged scale behind the lower jaw, a characteristic of this species.

10

The rhinoceros iguana, *Cyclura cornuta* (Iguanidae). Photo by Dr. S. A. Minton.

Ctenosaura hemilopha, a spiny iguana (Iguanidae). Photo by F. J. Dodd, Jr.

11

Introduction

In answering the inevitable question, "Why did you write this book?", I must refer to the current lack of factual, yet readable, material concerning the subject on the market. There simply is no book available to the general public that describes those lizards that can be easily kept by anyone from a schoolchild to an accomplished herpetologist and how to keep them.

In retrospect, I see that if such a book had been available to my parents or myself when I was a child, many anoles would have lived longer, happier lives. Hopefully this book will free other children, bewildered parents, schoolteachers, and the novice herpetologist from the worry of caring for these interesting, attractive, and delightful creatures.

Most people wonder what fascination these animals have for me and others infected with "herpetitis." Of course, some people have an instinctive love of all animals. Others could not have the companionship of a dog or cat and turned their interests toward smaller animals that required a minimum of care and space. The last group frankly just likes lizards. I'm afraid I fall into all three categories. As a teenager, I managed to outgrow a much loathed allergy and acquired a dog. I'm certain my parents held the belief that this would put an end to my reptilian tendencies, but such was not the case.

I must say at this point that I am not a professional herpetologist. As a matter of fact, my lizard-keeping is only a hobby. All the scientific and technical information I have acquired has been through books. Much practical information, however, has come from James Murphy, David Barker, and Lyndon Mitchell at the Dallas Marsalis Park Zoo.

Although I have drawn on several sources of information as to scientific names and habits, the bulk of the assembled information herein is from my own experience. It is my sincere wish that the reader will find usable facts and ideas here and will put them to good use.

Richard H. Wynne

Lizards in General

I have found that most people have preconceived notions as to what a reptile is. Unfortunately, very few really know what they are talking about. A list of "reptiles" might include anything from worms to frogs or armadillos.

A reptile, as a general rule, is a cold-blooded air-breathing vertebrate with scaly skin that lays shelled eggs on land. This rules out fish, birds, and mammals. The only other group of vertebrates that might be confused with reptiles is the amphibians. However, if the reader will refer to the following chart the distinction is easily seen:

REPTILES	AMPHIBIANS
Dry, scaly skin	Smooth, moist skin
Clawed feet	No claws on feet
Eggs laid in shells on land	Eggs laid in jellylike mass in water

At present, there are four living orders of reptiles:

(1) **Rhynchocephalia**—This order has only one surviving representative, a rare, endangered lizard-like animal known as the tuatara *(Sphenodon punctatus)* that lives on a few scattered islets off the coast of New Zealand.

(2) **Crocodylia**—The infamous alligators, crocodiles, caimans and gavials.

(3) **Chelonia**—The turtles, terrapins, and tortoises.

(4) **Squamata**—Depending upon which theory you personally ascribe to, there are two or three suborders in Squamata.

  (A) **Serpentes**—The snakes

  (B) **Sauria**—The lizards

    and

  (C) **Amphisbaenia**—The worm lizards

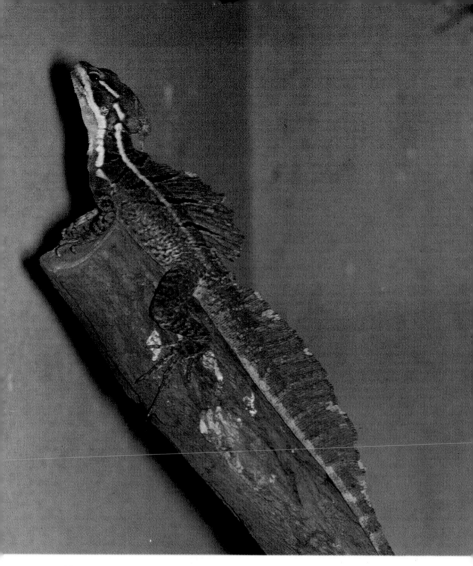

The brown basilisk, *Basiliscus basiliscus* (Iguanidae). Photo by H. Hansen, Aquarium Berlin.

Opposite:
Above: The green basilisk, *Basiliscus plumifrons* (Iguanidae). **Below:** *Laemanctus* sp., a cone-headed lizard (Iguanidae). Photo by A. Norman.

Some herpetologists consider this last group as a highly specialized form of lizard. Others believe it to be a completely distinct suborder. As I have had little first-hand experience with them, I remain unbiased. However, I do not include them in this book as the amateur will likely never encounter one in the field. Some fifteen other orders and numerous other suborders are represented by fossils, including the awesome dinosaurs. Lizards are in the order Squamata. This order encompasses nineteen families that will be broken down and described in the ensuing chapters.

GENERAL CHARACTERISTICS OF LIZARDS

A lizard is a reptile. It has dry, scaly skin, is cold-blooded, and has claws on its feet. It may possess four legs, two legs, or no legs at all. It may range in size from two inches to ten feet. Its scalation may be spiny and grotesque or smooth, shiny, and even iridescent. Its colors may blend with the surroundings so well that it is difficult to see even when in plain view, or it may be brightly hued in the most fanciful way one can imagine. It may live in the most parched and arid areas on earth or in the steaming jungles and rain-forests of the tropics. One species is even a marine animal. Another's range extends into the Arctic Circle. It may eat flowers, fruits, insects, other lizards, or even such large prey as wild hogs. Obviously, lizards are a diversified, highly adaptable, and quite successful form of life.

TEMPERATURE REQUIREMENTS OF LIZARDS

Lizards are cold-blooded. This means that their body temperature is not controlled internally but approximates that of their surroundings. Most lizards require a temperature of 70° to 90° Fahrenheit in order to function normally and digest their food. Desert species require higher temperatures and some can withstand (and may even require) conditions that would kill other animals, including man. The body temperature is regulated by periods of basking alternated with periods of cooling off, perhaps beneath a stone or bush.

ANATOMICAL CHARACTERISTICS OF LIZARDS

(1) *The Head Region*—All lizards possess eyes or remnants of eyes embedded beneath the skin. Most possess movable eyelids, one of

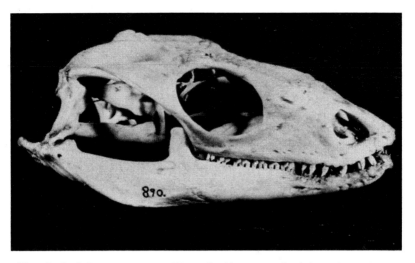

The skull of *Ctenosaura* sp. Photo by K. Lucas, Steinhart Aquarium.

the characteristics which distinguish them from the snakes. Others, like the geckos, night lizards, and pygopodids, have a transparent scale covering the eye, much in the fashion of a contact lens, rather than having movable eyelids. These clear scales are kept clean by licking them with the tongue. Many lizards rely on acute vision rather than the sense of smell for locating mates, enemies, and prey.

Many lizards have a highly developed sense of smell, possessing long forked tongues which are periodically protruded to "taste" the air. In reality, the tongue picks up minute particles in the air and transmits them to the Jacobson's organ in the roof of the mouth. This organ seems to be an extremely sensitive combination of the senses of taste and smell.

Lizards have an excellent sense of hearing. Most have an exposed eardrum or tympanum on each side of the head. Others have these organs covered by a thin layer of scales.

Teeth vary in size, shape, and placement among lizards. The placement is one of two types—pleurodont or acrodont. In *pleurodont* dentition the teeth are set on the inside of the jawbone. In *acrodont* the teeth are set on top of the jawbone. The shape of the teeth varies with the type of food consumed. Herbivorous species have flat grinding teeth; species that eat insects normally have

17

Corytophanes cristatus, a helmeted iguana (Iguanidae). Photo by A. Norman.

A fence swift, *Sceloporus orcutti* (Iguanidae). Photo by A. Norman.

Crotaphytus collaris, the collared lizard (Iguanidae). Photo by A. Norman. This species is now considered to be a complex of several very closely related species.

Gambelia wislizenii, the leopard lizard (Iguanidae). Photo by J. K. Langhammer.

Chameleons represent an extreme adaption in lizards. The prehensile tail, fused toes, and specialized eyes set them off from all other lizards. Photo by Dr. O. Klee.

Spinous dorsal crests are a common development in many lizard families, as are nuchal crests and nose humps or horns. Shown here is a sail-fin dragon, *Hydrosaurus*. Photo by G. Marcuse.

small pointed teeth in front and flattened grinders in the rear. Carnivorous species usually have sharply pointed teeth for holding and tearing prey, some even fang-like and resembling those of snakes. The poisonous varieties possess grooved teeth in the lower jaw that transfer the poison from the venom glands into the victim.

Many lizards have nuchal crests and bony helmet-like structures on the head. These are usually more pronounced in the male and are used for species recognition in seeking a mate or fighting a rival male. Others have bizarre ornamental horns or humps on the snout that serve the same purpose. Many species also bear a gular pouch or dewlap for species recognition and in some cases as a threat display. Old lizards of certain species may also develop heavy jowls.

Voices are rare among the lizards, and all most species can do is hiss. However, some species, notably the geckos, do possess vocal cords and can make squeaking or croaking sounds.

(2) *The Body Region*—The bodies of lizards vary greatly in shape. There are three basic configurations. Firstly, many lizards, in particular the skinks and lateral-fold lizards, have a long, cylindrical body. The lizards that are primarily arboreal usually have a body that is laterally flattened, sometimes almost absurdly so as in the

21

Phrynosoma coronatum, a horned lizard (Iguanidae). Photo by K. Lucas, Steinhart Aquarium.

Holbrookia maculata, an earless lizard (Iguanidae). Photo by J. F. Dodd, Jr.

Leiocephalus carinatus, the common curly-tailed lizard (Iguanidae). Photo by H. Hansen, Aquarium Berlin.

Anolis carolinensis, the green anole (Iguanidae). Photo by G. Marcuse.

chameleons. Lastly, those species that are primarily ground-dwellers usually have a body that is dorsoventrally flattened. Many species possess dorsal crests, most being used for species and sex recognition. However, recent studies show evidence that some of these crests are used as thermoregulatory devices for providing a greater surface area to expose to the sun for warming up.

Many people ask why lizards sit still for such long periods. The answer is really quite simple. Lizards are a primitive life form; they do not possess a four-chambered heart as mammals, including man, do, but have a heart with three incompletely divided chambers. This means that after a bout of activity there is a mixture of blood rich in oxygen and blood deficient in oxygen in the heart. Therefore, the lizard must rest to let his blood cells "get organized" again.

All lizards shed their skin periodically and need rocks or branches to rub the old skin loose. The old skin usually comes off in patches, and many species eat the sheds. Do not help the shedding process along unless the lizard has difficulty in the later stages.

(3) *The Tail Region*—Tails also vary greatly in lizards. The great majority are able to break off the tail to distract a predator. This broken portion usually writhes about convulsively for several minutes, giving the lizard plenty of time to escape. The tail will regenerate in time, but the regrown portion is usually shorter and of a different texture than the original. Occasionally the tail will not break completely and the result will be a forked tail. This may be unique and interesting to see, but it slows the lizard down and hinders its agility.

Certain lizards, primarily the chameleons, have developed a prehensile tail that is used as a fifth leg. These tails cannot be regenerated if broken. All lizards possessing prehensile tails are primarily arboreal in habit.

Other lizards have developed specialized tails for defensive purposes, some being rather heavy and covered with spines. Aquatic lizards have tails that are flattened laterally, some with tall caudal crests that are used to propel the lizards through the water. Still others have a long powerful tail that is used much in the manner of a bullwhip. A blow from such a tail is usually enough to dissuade an attacker.

Lizard Family Tree

This section is intended to give the reader a general overview of the nineteen families of lizards and the geographical ranges they inhabit.

I. TEIIDAE

Also known as the whiptails or teiids, this family includes approximately 50 genera and some 200 species. They range from the United States to Central America and Argentina. Arboreal, aquatic, and land-dwelling species are known, living in deserts, rain-forests, and cool mountain jungles.

II. LACERTIDAE

As the Old World counterparts of the New World teiids, the lacertids fill the same ecological niches in Europe, Africa, and Asia as the teiids do in the Americas. There are 20 genera with more than 200 species. Like the teiids, the lacertids occupy a wide variety of habitats and include among their number one lizard that lives inside the Arctic Circle.

III. IGUANIDAE

The Iguanidae is a large family comprised of over 50 genera and more than 700 species. The iguanids range from North America through South America, with a few representatives on Madagascar, Fiji, and Tonga. Like the teiids and lacertids, the iguanids are at home in many habitats.

IV. AGAMIDAE

The agamids and iguanids display a marked tendency toward convergent evolution. That is, for almost every agamid occupying a particular habitat in the Old World, an iguanid of similar ap-

Acanthosaura crucigera, a mountain dragon (Agamidae). Photo by A. Norman.

Gonocephalus grandis, a tree dragon (Agamidae). Photo by J. Bridges.

Physignathus cocincinus, the Chinese water dragon (Agamidae).

Agama nupta, a common agama (Agamidae). Photo by Dr. S. A. Minton.

pearance and/or habits may be found in a like habitat in the New World. Some agamids are so similar to iguanids that the only anatomical difference is in the placement of the teeth. The teeth of the agamids are acrodont, the teeth of the iguanids are pleurodont. The agamids are found in Africa, Europe, Asia, and Australia; there are about 35 genera and some 300 species.

V. VARANIDAE

This family is strictly an Old World family with one genus, *Varanus,* made up of over 30 species. These are the monitors and goannas, largest of all lizards. They occupy deserts, rivers and streams, trees, and other diverse habitats. They inhabit Africa, Asia, and Australia.

VI. SCINCIDAE

The skinks are a large family of lizards with 50 genera and about 800 species. They inhabit every continent, excluding Antarctica, and live in every habitat imaginable.

VII. CORDYLIDAE

The cordylids or girdle-tails are an African family restricted to the subsahara area of that continent. There are 10 genera with around 80 species. Most cordylids favor dry, rocky habitats and are very tolerant of temperature fluctuations.

VIII. GEKKONIDAE

The geckos are a large family with 83 genera and nearly 700 species. The geckos, like the skinks, live on every continent. These lizards are highly specialized with unusual scalation on their feet that enables them to climb vertical surfaces with ease and even to walk across ceilings. The majority do not possess movable eyelids.

IX. ANGUINIDAE

The anguinids or lateral-fold lizards are an interesting group occurring in both the Old and New Worlds. There are 8 genera with about 70 species. The name lateral-fold lizard comes from the heavy folds of skin along the sides of the body in several members of the family.

Detail of the head of a gecko. Notice the lidless eye and the vertical pupil divided into distinct "pin holes," common features of the family Gekkonidae. Photo by Dr. H. R. Axelrod.

X. CHAMAELEONTIDAE

The true chameleons are an Old World family ranging from Europe to Africa and Asia, with the majority of species being African. There are 2 or 3 genera with about 90 species currently described. These lizards are unique in many ways and many herpetologists feel that they should be placed in a suborder of their own, parallel with the other lizards.

XI. XANTUSIDAE

The xantusids are usually referred to as the night lizards due to their nocturnal habits. These small lizards are usually nocturnal and are all from the New World. There are 4 genera with a total of 12 species. They occupy a wide range of habitats from deserts to humid tropical areas.

XII. XENOSAURIDAE

This is a small and poorly known family made up of 2 genera, one in the Old World and one in the New World, with fewer than a dozen species. One genus is from China and the other is found in Mexico.

Draco lineatus, a flying dragon (Agamidae). Photo by Dr. S. A. Minton. The "wings" are normally folded to the sides and are not clearly visible.

Calotes emma, a bloodsucker (Agamidae). Photo by A. Norman.

Chlamydosaurus kingii, the frilled dragon (Agamidae). Photo by H. Frauca. This is the defensive pose, with the frill extended and the mouth opened.

Moloch horridus, the moloch (Agamidae). Photo by K. Lucas, Steinhart Aquarium.

Skulls of two teiids. Above is that of a tegu, *Tupinambis;* below is that of a caiman lizard, *Dracaena.* Notice the much heavier teeth and lower jaw of *Dracaena,* both adaptations for crushing snails. Photos by K. Lucas, Steinhart Aquarium.

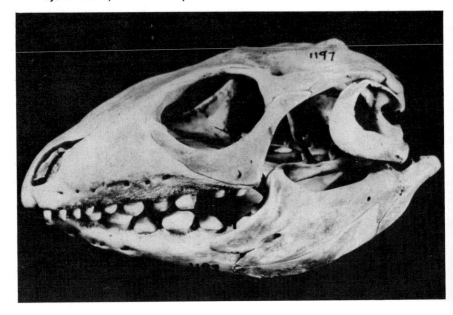

Skulls of *Cyclura cornuta,* an iguanid (above), and *Chamaeleo melleri,*
a chameleon (below). Photos by K. Lucas, Steinhart Aquarium.

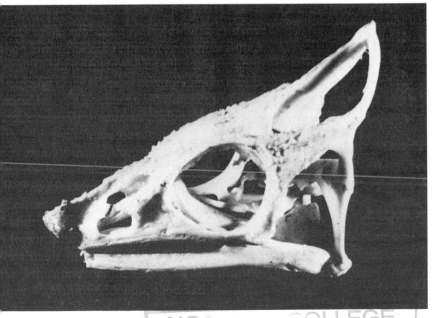

XIII. HELODERMATIDAE

This family includes the only known poisonous lizards. The group is strictly American with but one genus and two species. These beaded lizards, as they are popularly called, prefer dry, rocky habitats.

XIV. LANTHANOTIDAE

The earless monitors are represented by only one species found in Borneo. It is a little known and rarely seen animal, nocturnal and semiaquatic in its habits.

XV. PYGOPODIDAE

The snake-lizards are a small family comprised of about seven genera and fewer than 20 species restricted to New Guinea and Australia. Most are ground-dwellers and all are serpentine with no visible front limbs. The hind limbs are much reduced and resemble flaps of skin.

XVI. DIBAMIDAE

This group is comprised of a single genus with 3 species, all of which are legless burrowers with reduced eyes and no visible ear openings. They are from the Far East and Indonesia.

XVII. ANNIELLIDAE

The shovel-snouted legless lizards live only in North America. They prefer coastal areas with sandy soil that facilitates burrowing. There are 2 species in the one genus.

XVIII. FEYLINIDAE

This group of legless and earless burrowing lizards is from Africa. There is one genus and 4 species. This family is commonly united with Scincidae.

XIX. ANELYTROPSIDAE

This is a rare group of blind, legless burrowers found only a few times in Mexico. There is only one genus with a single species. This family may in time be united with Dibamidae.

Teiidae

The Teiids

The teiids fill the same ecological niche in the New World as the lacertas do in the Old World. Many species are so similar, in fact, that only a professional herpetologist can determine which family they belong to by studying minor anatomical differences. Although teiids vary greatly in size, color, and scalation, they all maintain a somewhat standard lizard shape with the exception of several small burrowing species in Central and South America.

All have moderately long tails that are either cylindrical or flattened laterally in aquatic species. The tails may be broken in an emergency and regenerated. There is never a dorsal crest, although some species have heavily keeled or raised scales on the back. There is also no dewlap, but some of the larger species may develop fat throat pouches and jowls. Teiids are incapable of changing their color except during the breeding season, when the coloration of males may become more intense. Teiids are egg-layers, some laying in such bizarre places as in the mounds of termites. The sense of smell is particularly acute in teiids, the tongue being long and forked in most species.

COMMON TEGU
(Tupinambis teguixin)

DISTRIBUTION: South America.

LENGTH: 48″ maximum, 36″ average.

DESCRIPTION: Originally there were three separate species of tegu described: the black tegu *(Tupinambis teguixin),* the golden tegu *(Tupinambis nigropunctatus),* and the red tegu *(Tupinambis rufescens).* The golden tegu was found to be a racial variant of the black tegu and is now considered to be the same species. The red tegu is not as commonly seen in captivity but may be kept like the common tegu. The common tegu

35

is a large animal, rather squat-bodied and heavy compared to other lizards of the same length. It is commonly a glossy black with scattered white or gold spots. The tail is strongly marked with alternating broad black and white bands in the young that fade with age. The belly is the same color as the spots on the body, mottled with black or bluish black. Old males tend to develop heavy jowls, as will fattened specimens of both sexes. The legs are powerful, and these lizards are quite fast. The tail is long and cylindrical and may be broken and regenerated.

HABITAT: A jungle animal with a preference for open spaces in which to bask.

CAGE: Large specimens do best in a simple display cage. Use a large cage with newspapers or pine chips for flooring material. Young specimens do well in a rain-forest cage.

TEMPERATURE RANGE: 75-85°F.; enjoys high temperatures.

FOOD AND WATER: Mice, rats, chickens, insects, sweet fruits, lizards, and an occasional egg. A large pan of water is essential for soaking and drinking, and a drip system is beneficial.

SPECIAL NEEDS: Plenty of sunlight mandatory. Vitamin supplements and bone meal should be added to all food.

YOUNG: Egg-layers that will lay anywhere in a cage. They lay in termite mounds in the wild. Young 6-8" at hatching.

RELATED SPECIES: The red tegu is a brick-red or brown species marked with white and cream.

JUNGLE RUNNERS
(Ameiva spp.*)*

DISTRIBUTION: Central and South America; introduced into Florida Keys.

LENGTH: 12-24"; average 15".

DESCRIPTION: Ameivas are alert, nervous lizards with highly variable color patterns. As a general rule most are brown anteriorly and green posteriorly with a profusion of spots or bars forming irregular lateral rows. The belly of males is often a turquoise blue, white in females. Ameivas possess heavily clawed forefeet that are used in digging and burrowing, which occupies a great deal of their time. The males will develop thick jowls as they age, much as do tegus. The tails of ameivas break very easily, so handle with care.

HABITAT: Ameivas come from a variety of habitats. The majority of them come from jungles and open grasslands. The darker, more greenish animals are generally jungle animals. The lighter, tan to brown animals are usually grassland inhabitants.

CAGE: Grassland species will do well in a woodland cage. Jungle species will thrive in a rain-forest cage.

TEMPERATURE RANGE: 75-85°F.

FOOD AND WATER: Primary diet is insects and spiders. Some small mice and lizards may be taken as well as sweet fruits. Ameivas enjoy soaking, so a large pan of water is essential, as is a drip system.

SPECIAL NEEDS: Sunlight is essential as are vitamin supplements and bone meal.

YOUNG: Egg-layers, prefer moist earth for laying. Young 3-5" at hatching.

RELATED SPECIES: Racerunners are often very similar to ameivas and may be found in the same areas. One general difference is the shorter snout of the racerunners.

RACERUNNERS
(Cnemidophorus spp.)

DISTRIBUTION: North and Central America.

LENGTH: 8-15".

DESCRIPTION: Racerunners or whiptails are agile, fast-moving lizards of open fields and rocky plains. They are slim-bodied and long-tailed lizards, most attractively marked with light stripes or spots on a darker ground color. As in the ameivas, the males may be strongly marked with bright blue on the ventral surfaces. Similarly, the forefeet are heavily clawed for digging and the tail is equally fragile. These animals are of special interest to herpetologists, for several species appear to be made up of only females that reproduce parthenogenetically. Racerunners and ameivas both become accustomed to the presence of humans and become extremely bold—almost friendly.

HABITAT: Normally found in dry, open areas that allow plenty of uninterrupted running room. They prefer areas that have an abundance of rocks and bushes for hiding places.

CAGE: Woodland or desert.

TEMPERATURE RANGE: 75-85°F.

FOOD AND WATER: Insects, spiders, and smaller lizards are the primary diet. Very little plant material is consumed. Racerunners enjoy bathing and appreciate a large container of water. Drip system is beneficial.

SPECIAL NEEDS: Racerunners need a great deal of direct sunlight. Vitamin supplements and bone meal should be added to food occasionally.

YOUNG: Egg-layers, prefer moist earth or sand for laying. Young 2½-3″ at hatching.

RELATED SPECIES: Ameivas are quite similar but larger with longer snouts.

CAIMAN LIZARD
(Dracaena guianensis)

DISTRIBUTION: South America.

LENGTH: 36-48″.

DESCRIPTION: True to its name, the caiman lizard resembles the South American version of the alligator, the caiman. The body is covered with heavy armored plates. The head is large and powerfully muscled, with large flat teeth used to crush the snails and clams on which it feeds. The basic color is dark brown with a tinge of rust and green on the head and neck. The tail is broad and flattened for swimming. Caiman lizards are excellent swimmers and make use of their ability in their natural habitat, the "igapo" forests of South America.

HABITAT: Caiman lizards live in swampy forests called "igapo" by local Indians. This ground will not support humans, and as a result these animals are rarely collected.

Detail of the head scalation of *Dracaena guianensis*. Photo by G. Marcuse.

CAGE: Only an extremely large cage is suitable for these lizards. The cage should be equally divided between land and water. A few inches of blasting sand should be placed on the bottom of the water area and a subsurface filter installed to keep the water clean.

TEMPERATURE RANGE: 80-90°F.; water-78°F.

FOOD: Caiman lizards eat only hard-shelled snails and clams; substitutes are usually not accepted. I do not recommend keeping these lizards in captivity.

SPECIAL NEEDS: Sunlight beneficial. Vitamins and bone meal should be added to all food.

YOUNG: Egg-layers, will lay anywhere in cage. Often lay in termite mounds in the wild. Young 7-9" at hatching.

RELATED SPECIES: None, although tegus may look somewhat similar.

ROUGH TEIID
(Echinosaura horridus)

DISTRIBUTION: South America.

LENGTH: 4-6".

DESCRIPTION: Many small teiids live on the rain-forest floor in South America. The rough teiid's habits and diet are fairly typical and will be used as the example here. This animal is a slow-moving, bright-eyed little creature that hides among the leaf litter and moss on the jungle floor. The snout is peculiarly pointed. The back is divided into two rows of large plates with rows of small keeled scales between the plates on either side. The tail is covered with small keeled scales and is rather stiff. The rough teiid has the disquieting habit of playing dead when approached, to the extent of becoming stiff, closing its eyes, and ceasing breathing.

HABITAT: Lives among fallen leaves and other debris. Rarely basks or climbs. Extremely secretive.

CAGE: Rain-forest with plenty of cover.

TEMPERATURE RANGE: 75-85°F.

FOOD AND WATER: Small insects are the sole food. A small water dish should be supplied and a drip system is mandatory as these lizards are used to a moist environment.

SPECIAL NEEDS: Not especially dependent on sunlight. Vitamins and bone meal should be added to food occasionally.

YOUNG: Egg-layers, prefer moist earth for laying. Young 3-5" at hatching.

RELATED SPECIES: No other teiids have the strong scalation of this animal, although many have the same habits.

Lacertidae

The Lacertas

The lacertas fill the same ecological niche in the Old World as the teiids do in the New World. Minor anatomical differences are the only factors that keep these two families separate. The lacertas are often called the "true lizards" because they all maintain a fairly typical lizard-like shape. Most lacertas have strong legs and, although some species have legs that are somewhat reduced in size, there are no legless varieties.

Most possess long round tails that are easily broken and regenerated. The scales are usually smooth but bear keels in some species. Desert species often have fringe-like structures on the toes for better traction on loose sand. Like the teiids, no lacertas have dewlaps or dorsal crests. Larger specimens may have jowls or throat pouches, however. The sense of smell is highly developed; the tongues are long and forked. The lacertas are comprised of both egg-laying and live-bearing species.

Detail of the head scalation of a typical lacertid, *Lacerta viridis.* Photo by Muller-Schmida.

EYED LIZARD
(Lacerta lepida)

DISTRIBUTION: Europe east to Asia Minor.

LENGTH: 18-30".

DESCRIPTION: This animal is one of the most beautifully marked lizards. The ground color is grass green in the male, light olive in the female. The male has a row of vivid blue spots outlined in black along each side. The female's spots are more subdued. The tail is long and fragile. Eyed lizards are the largest member of the lacerta family and will not hesitate to fight off larger predators such as dogs and cats. If the situation becomes too intense these lizards will climb trees or swim to escape.

HABITAT: Open rocky fields along the borders of forests. Extremely active runners and climbers. Bask frequently.

CAGE: Woodland.

TEMPERATURE RANGE: 70-85°F.

FOOD AND WATER: Insects, spiders, small rodents and reptiles, some fruits, flowers, and plant material make up the diet. Supply a large container of water for drinking and bathing.

SPECIAL NEEDS: Sunlight mandatory. Add vitamins and bone meal to all plant food.

YOUNG: Egg-layers, prefer sandy soil for laying. Young 3-4" at hatching.

RELATED SPECIES: Green lizards are similar but lack the blue spots.

GREEN LIZARD
(Lacerta viridis)

DISTRIBUTION: Europe east to Asia Minor.

LENGTH: 12-18".

DESCRIPTION: The green lizard is a beautiful animal. The male is a bright emerald green with a bluish throat and golden belly; the female is grass green with a white ventral surface. Occasional individuals may have white striping on the back.

These lizards are very agile creatures with strong claws and a long fragile tail. It is extremely territorial, and disputes between rival males are commonplace. The green lizard is an excellent climber and basks frequently in the lower branches of trees.

HABITAT: Inhabits meadows along the borders of woodlands, often venturing into the yards of homes where food is abundant.

CAGE: Woodland.

TEMPERATURE RANGE: 70-85°F.

FOOD AND WATER: Insects, spiders, small rodents and lizards, and sweet fruits and other plant material make up the diet. Water should be supplied in a large container. A drip system is probably beneficial.

SPECIAL NEEDS: Sunlight essential. Add vitamins and bone meal to all plant material.

YOUNG: Egg-layers, prefer sheltered sandy soil for laying. Young 3-4" at hatching.

RELATED SPECIES: Eyed lizard is similar but has a row of blue spots down the sides.

COMMON LIZARD
(Lacerta vivipara)

DISTRIBUTION: Europe to eastern Asia.

LENGTH: 6-10".

DESCRIPTION: Common lizards are nervous, quick, and elusive animals occupying a huge range and living in many habitats. Colors vary from sandy brown to solid black with many racial variations. Most will have a spotted pattern dorsally and be unmarked ventrally. The tail is very fragile and is discarded easily. Common lizards are almost unique among the lacertas because they are ovoviviparous. In other words, the infants are born fully developed encased in an embryonic sac that they break out of immediately.

HABITAT: Fields near forests; often found on garden fences and the walls of houses. Ranges as far north as the Arctic Circle.

CAGE: Woodland.

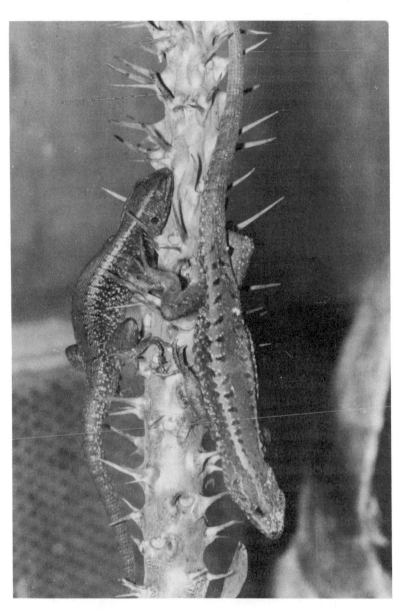

Wall lizards, *Lacerta muralis*. This species and several others (including the ruins lizard, *L. sicula)* are now placed by many herpetologists in the separate genus *Podarcis,* which is based mostly in skeletal characters not visible externally. Photo by H. Hansen, Aquarium Berlin.

TEMPERATURE RANGE: 70-80°F.

FOOD AND WATER: Insects, spiders, and some plant material make up the primary diet. A small water dish should be supplied for drinking. Drip system optional.

SPECIAL NEEDS: Sunlight for basking mandatory; some vitamins and minerals should be added to food occasionally.

YOUNG: Young born alive in sacs; females will drop young anywhere. Young 1½-2½" at birth.

RELATED SPECIES: Wall lizard, ruins lizard.

WALL LIZARD

(Lacerta muralis)

DISTRIBUTION: Europe, introduced colonies in northeastern United States.

LENGTH: 6-8".

DESCRIPTION: Wall lizards are small, fast-moving lizards common in southern Europe. These brightly marked animals are olive brown to light green on the back with black spots forming an irregular pattern. The belly is often reddish with black mottling on the throat. The tail is long and fragile and the claws are sharp and long for agility in climbing. These lizards were once quite common in the vineyards of France, but the increased use of pesticides has reduced their numbers. A small breeding population has been living in the Philadelphia area for many years.

HABITAT: Common in meadows along the edges of woods; often found in close proximity to man on garden fences and the walls of houses.

CAGE: Woodland.

TEMPERATURE RANGE: 70-80°F.

FOOD AND WATER: Insects, spiders, and some plant material are the primary diet. A small container of water should be supplied for drinking. Drip system optional.

SPECIAL NEEDS: Sunlight essential for frequent basking. Vitamins may be added to diet as needed.

Egg-layers, prefer shady soil for laying. Young 1½-2½"
at hatching.

RELATED SPECIES: Common lizard, ruins lizard.

RUINS LIZARD
(Lacerta sicula)

DISTRIBUTION: Europe.

LENGTH: 6-8".

DESCRIPTION: A small nervous lizard that moves with blurring
speed. They move up vertical surfaces such as trees and walls
as quickly as they traverse level ground. The ground color
may be green or olive with a network of black markings across
the back. The appearance is quite similar to the wall lizard but
lacks the black markings on the throat. The subspecies may be
various solid colors such as green, olive, or even black. The
species possesses a long thin tail which is lost quite easily.

HABITAT: Rocky hillsides and meadows. Often seen crawling
among the ruins of Pompeii, hence the name. Sometimes called
the lava lizard.

CAGE: Woodland.

TEMPERATURE RANGE: 75-80°F.

FOOD AND WATER: Insects, spiders, and some plant material
make up the basic diet. A small container of water is necessary
for drinking. Drip system is optional.

SPECIAL NEEDS: Sunlight is essential for basking. Vitamins
may be added to food if needed.

YOUNG: Egg-layers, prefer sandy soil for laying. Young 2-3" at
hatching.

RELATED SPECIES: Common lizard, wall lizard.

Iguanidae

The Iguanas

The iguanas fill the same general niche in the New World as the agamas do in the Old World. The only real difference between the families is in the placement of the teeth. In iguanas the teeth are set on the inside of the jawbone. This is known as pleurodont dentition. The agamas have acrodont dentition, the teeth being set on top of the jawbone.

Iguanas are extremely variable in appearance, some being adorned with large dorsal crests, dewlaps, spiny tails and bodies, prehensile tails, extraordinary color-changing abilities, and eyes that move independently as in the chameleons. Most have strong legs used for running and strong claws for digging or climbing. Some possess special pads on the toes that enable them to scale vertical surfaces. There are no legless species. The tail is usually breakable and may be regenerated. Most iguanas rely more on keen eyesight than the sense of smell in locating prey. The tongue is usually short and fleshy. The iguanas are egg-layers.

COMMON IGUANA
(Iguana iguana)

DISTRIBUTION: Central and South America.

LENGTH: 48-78"; average 60".

DESCRIPTION: The common or green iguana is a large impressive animal reminiscent of the dinosaurs. The main color is bright green with a tinge of blue on the head and neck. The underside is light green to dirty white. There is usually a series of broad black bands alternating with green encircling the tail. These may be more pronounced in young specimens. A large dewlap, which may hang down five inches in a large male, is present. There is a tall dorsal crest beginning in the nuchal area and continuing well down the tail. The toes are heavily clawed; these lizards are primarily arboreal and use the claws in climbing.

HABITAT: Jungle trees; iguanas rarely descend, although when threatened they may leap several yards to the ground or dive into shallow water to escape.

CAGE: Young specimens can be kept healthy in a rain-forest cage. Large specimens are best allowed the run of the house unless a huge terrarium with small trees and large branches can be supplied.

TEMPERATURE RANGE: 80-90°F.

FOOD AND WATER: Adults are mainly herbivorous; a variety of fruits, vegetables, and flowers should be offered. Occasionally an insect or mouse will be taken. Young specimens are mainly insectivorous but will take some plant material. A large container of water with a drip system is essential.

SPECIAL NEEDS: Sunlight is essential, as are vitamins and bone meal.

YOUNG: Egg-layers, rarely breed in captivity. Young 8-9" at hatching.

RELATED SPECIES: None. Rhinoceros iguanas and spiny iguanas are similar in appearance.

RHINOCEROS IGUANAS
(Cyclura spp.)

DISTRIBUTION: West Indies.

LENGTH: 36-48".

DESCRIPTION: The genus *Cyclura* is characterized by large, heavy, squat bodies, thick tails, heavy jowls, and a short dorsal crest. The jaws are extremely powerful and are lined with large crushing teeth. The true rhinoceros iguana *(Cyclura cornuta)* has two small horns on its snout. These large iguanids are remarkably nimble for their bulk and can be dangerous when aroused. The color is usually a shade of light brown or green dorsally and dirty white ventrally. Most species are ground-dwellers. However, young specimens of most species are good climbers as well.

HABITAT: Most species live on scattered islands throughout the Caribbean and favor dry, rocky habitats which allow for basking. Others, such as *Cyclura figginsii* and *Cyclura macklaeyii,* require more moisture and may be found on the outskirts of jungles.

CAGE: Only a very large cage is suitable for these lizards. A woodland cage with very few furnishings is good.

TEMPERATURE RANGE: 80-90°F.

FOOD AND WATER: Rhinoceros iguanas are omnivorous. Insects, rodents, birds, lizards, fruits, vegetables, and other plant material will all be readily taken. A large basin of water should be supplied along with a large drip system.

SPECIAL NEEDS: Sunlight is essential. Vitamins and bone meal should be added to all plant food.

YOUNG: Egg-layers, prefer shady soil for laying. Young 6-7" at hatching.

RELATED SPECIES: All rhinoceros iguanas are similar. Some species resemble the common iguana and the spiny iguana.

COMMENT: Several species of this genus are now considered endangered and may not be kept.

SPINY IGUANAS
(*Ctenosaura* spp.)

DISTRIBUTION: Central America.

LENGTH: 24-36".

DESCRIPTION: Spiny iguanas are lively long-tailed lizards fond of basking and digging. Most maintain a vicious disposition even as youngsters, and large angry specimens can actually be dangerous. The ground color is dark brown to gray or black depending on the species or subspecies. Most specimens are mottled with black dorsally. The belly is usually dirty white. The tail is ringed with spiny scales that give the animals their name. There is a very short dorsal crest on most specimens. However, *Ctenosaura similis* has a rather tall crest.

HABITAT: Common around ruins in Central America. Fond of basking on stone walls and in the lower branches of large trees along the borders of forests.

Left: A Cayman Islands rhinoceros iguana, *Cyclura caymanensis*. The species of *Cyclura* are poorly understood, and the name *caymanensis* is often seen used as a subspecies of other species. Photo by Muller-Schmida. **Below:** *Ctenosaura acanthura,* one of the several confusing species of spiny iguanas. Photo by the author.

Two views of a male *Sceloporus occidentalis* from California. Male fence swifts commonly have bright blue to blackish patches under the throat and on the sides of the belly as shown below. Photos by K. Lucas, Steinhart Aquarium.

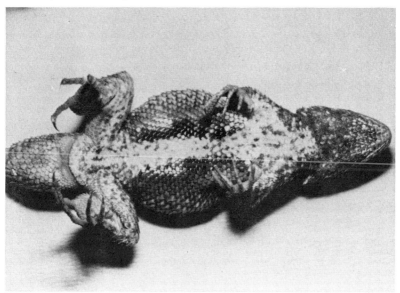

CAGE: Woodland.

TEMPERATURE RANGE: 80-90°F.

FOOD AND WATER: Spiny iguanas are omnivorous but prefer animal food. The natural diet consists of insects, spiders, lizards, rodents, fruits, and leaves. Spiny iguanas have a low requirement for drinking water, but supply a small dish for soaking.

SPECIAL NEEDS: Sunlight is mandatory. Vitamins and bone meal should be added to all plant food.

YOUNG: Egg-layers, prefer sandy soil for laying. Young 6-7" at hatching.

RELATED SPECIES: Common iguanas and rhinoceros iguanas are similar, especially when young.

BASILISKS
(*Basiliscus* spp.)

DISTRIBUTION: Central America.

LENGTH: Green basilisk *(Basiliscus plumifrons)* 36"; brown basilisk *(Basiliscus basiliscus)* 24-30"; banded basilisk *(Basiliscus vittatus)* 18-24".

DESCRIPTION: The basilisks are a unique group of iguanids noted for their bizarre crests. The green basilisk is normally bright emerald green with blue and black spots. The eye is a bright yellow. The male has a double crest and a high "sail" extending down the back and onto the tail. The tail itself is broad and flattened for swimming. The female has a small knob on the back of the head but no crest. The brown or common basilisk is a brown animal marked with a light stripe down each side. There is a single head crest and a tall dorsal sail extending onto the tail. The eye is brown. The female is similar but lacks the sail. The banded basilisk is a smaller animal with less outstanding features. The basic ground color is gray-brown with several black bands down the sides. The male has a large head crest and a short dorsal crest. The female has a small knob on the head and no dorsal crest. Basilisks have the unique ability to run across the surface of water for several yards before falling in and swimming. They normally run on their hind legs.

HABITAT: Jungle trees and undergrowth near a body of water. Banded basilisks are sometimes found among the ruins of ancient buildings in Mexico. They bask frequently on limbs overhanging water.

CAGE: Rain-forest.

TEMPERATURE RANGE: 80-90ºF.

FOOD AND WATER: Basilisks require mostly animal food. Include insects, small mice, and some sweet fruits in their diet. A large pan of water should be supplied with a drip system.

SPECIAL NEEDS: Sunlight is essential. Vitamins and bone meal should be added to food periodically.

YOUNG: Egg-layers, prefer rotting logs or sheltered moist soil for laying. Young 4-6″ at hatching.

RELATED SPECIES: Cone-headed lizards, helmeted iguanas, and sail-fin dragons are similar.

CONE-HEADED LIZARDS
(*Laemanctus* spp.)

DISTRIBUTION: Central America.

LENGTH: 18-24″.

DESCRIPTION: These lizards are slender, long-legged arboreal animals with long thin tails. There are several species all very similar in color and appearance. The color is light green to olive. There is usually a black streak from the eye down onto the neck. The belly is immaculate white or yellow-white. There is no dorsal crest as in the basilisks, to which they are related, but there is a small cone-shaped protrusion on the back of the head. The tail is fragile and may make up two-thirds to three-fourths of the total length. The cone-headed lizards are strictly tree dwellers, rarely descending to the ground.

HABITAT: Found in dense jungles, usually high in the trees.

CAGE: Rain-forest.

53

TEMPERATURE RANGE: 80-90°F.

FOOD AND WATER: Insects, spiders, small lizards, and rodents. They are said to consume some plant material but I have seen no physical evidence of this. A moderate-sized water container should be supplied for drinking.

SPECIAL NEEDS: Sunlight is essential for basking. Vitamins and bone meal should be added to food periodically.

YOUNG: Egg-layers, prefer moist soil or humus beneath the roots of trees for laying. Young 4-5″ at hatching.

RELATED SPECIES: Basilisks and helmeted iguanas are similar as are the sail-fin dragons.

HELMETED IGUANAS
(*Corytophanes* spp.)

DISTRIBUTION: Central America.

LENGTH: 12-16″.

DESCRIPTION: Helmeted iguanas are unusual long-legged lizards with an enormous head crest. These animals also have a throat pouch which is distensible. This gives the lizard's head the appearance of an exaggerated arrowhead. There are three species, of which *Corytophanes cristatus* is the most commonly imported. These lizards range in color from rich chocolate brown through olive to gray with lighter spots and mottlings. The thin tail is roughly one and a half times the body length and occasionally is marked with alternating light and dark bands. The overall appearance of the animal is reminiscent of a frog. Helmeted iguanas are also very similar in habits to the mountain dragons. I feel that these groups of lizards show definite signs of convergent evolution. They occupy the same basic niche in their respective natural habitats.

HABITAT: Found in the forests of Central America. Usually found in low bushes or in the lower branches of small trees. Fairly secretive in habits and not particularly active.

CAGE: Rain-forest with plenty of cover.

TEMPERATURE RANGE: 75-85°F.

FOOD AND WATER: Readily accepts most insects and spiders,

young mice, and small food lizards. Also eats earthworms, which may be the natural diet. A large water dish and drip system are needed.

SPECIAL NEEDS: Some sunlight is beneficial. Will decline rapidly in captivity if not supplied with plenty of vitamins and bone meal.

YOUNG: Egg-layers, prefer moist earth or humus for laying. Young 3-4" at hatching.

RELATED SPECIES: Basilisks, cone-headed lizards and mountain dragons are similar in appearance and habits.

FENCE SWIFTS
(*Sceloporus* spp.)

DISTRIBUTION: North and Central America.

LENGTH: 6-14".

DESCRIPTION: There are many species of *Sceloporus* that live in a variety of habitats. As a general rule most are lively, alert, fast-moving lizards with a tail as long as or slightly longer than the body. Most have overlapping scales on the neck, body, and tail that give the lizards a spiny appearance. There are some exceptions to this general appearance that look more like a side-blotched lizard. Most fence swifts or spiny swifts are a shade of brown or gray with dark bars across the back and in some species a dark "collar" around the neck. Males often have bright blue patches on the throat and belly. Several species are brightly colored with blue, red, orange, green, or purple markings. The tail is detachable.

HABITAT: The desert species are found in the southwestern United States and Mexico, preferring rocky areas. Woodland species prefer cooler climates and may be found well up in trees. They also may be seen clambering over garden walls and fences, hence the common name. Grassland species are normally less spiny and prefer open areas that permit plenty of running. Bask frequently and are very active.

CAGE: Desert for desert species; woodland for woodland species; woodland with sparse cover for grassland species.

TEMPERATURE RANGE: 70-85°F. for woodland and grassland species; 85-95°F. for desert species.

FOOD AND WATER: Insects and spiders are the main diet, but larger species may also include small vertebrates in their diet. Some plant material may also be taken. A small dish of water should be supplied for desert species and a large pan should be provided to the others. Drip system optional.

SPECIAL NEEDS: Sunlight mandatory. Fence swifts are extremely hardy and require little special care. Some vitamin supplements and bone meal should be added to food occasionally.

YOUNG: Some species are live-bearers, some are egg-layers. The egg-layers prefer sandy soil beneath a tree or bush for laying. Young 1-2½″ at hatching.

RELATED SPECIES: Many species of fence lizards are quite similar to each other and are difficult to identify precisely. Side-blotched lizards and sand lizards are also similar.

DESERT IGUANA
(Dipsosaurus dorsalis)

DISTRIBUTION: Western North America.

LENGTH: 12-18″; average 15″.

DESCRIPTION: One of the larger North American lizards. The body is fairly stout, which may be accentuated by the habit of inflating the body with air when disturbed. There is a very short dorsal crest. The tail is long, round, and thick; it is detachable and will regenerate if broken. The gular region bears a dewlap. The legs are thick and powerful; the desert iguana is a speedy runner. The basic color is light brown broken with irregular bars and spots of white, and the sides and belly are pure white. From a distance the overall effect is that of a snow-white lizard. This coloration blends in well with the sandy and rocky areas the desert iguana inhabits. Basks frequently atop rocks.

HABITAT: The driest, hottest areas in the American Southwest. Prefers flat areas with sparse shrubbery and sandy soil. Capable of withstanding incredibly high temperatures.

CAGE: Desert.

TEMPERATURE RANGE: 90-100°F.; cannot digest food below 90°F.

FOOD AND WATER: The main diet is the tender leaves, flowers, and fruits of desert plants. Insects are also taken. Desert iguanas do not drink standing water in nature, but supply a small dish.

SPECIAL NEEDS: Sunlight and dry heat mandatory. The slightest amount of moisture will cause a fast decline. Vitamins should be added to all plant food.

YOUNG: Egg-layers, dig long complex tunnels in the desert sand for laying. Young 3-4" at hatching.

RELATED SPECIES: Resembles a young common iguana. Shares certain characteristics with the chuckwalla.

CHUCKWALLA
(Sauromalus obesus)

DISTRIBUTION: Western North America.

LENGTH: 12-18"; average 16".

DESCRIPTION: Chuckwallas are the second largest native lizards found in the United States. They are extremely stout, with a dorsoventrally flattened body. The tail is fairly short and rounded with circular rings of scales bearing minute keels; the skin feels like sandpaper. The chuckwalla defends itself by crawling into a rock crevice, inflating its body with air, and wedging itself in tightly. It can only be removed by puncturing it and killing it or by using a crowbar to pry open the rocks. Chuckwallas vary in color from subspecies to subspecies. One color phase is completely dark blackish brown. Another has a black head and shoulders, orange-red body, and white tail ringed with black bands. A final phase lacks the rings. These sun-loving lizards bask frequently atop desert boulders that allow them a full view of their surroundings.

HABITAT: The most arid areas of the American Southwest. Prefer rocky country which provides both food and shelter.

CAGE: Desert.

TEMPERATURE RANGE: 90-100°F.

FOOD AND WATER: The main diet is desert leaves, flowers, and fruits, and it is especially partial to the fruits of the cactus plants, especially the prickly pear. Insects occasionally are taken as well. In nature, chuckwallas do not normally have drinking water available, but supply a small dish.

SPECIAL NEEDS: Sunlight and dry heat are mandatory. Vitamins and bone meal should be added to all plant food.

YOUNG: Egg-layers, prefer sandy soil for laying. Young 3-4" at hatching.

RELATED SPECIES: Very similar in habits to the desert iguana.

GREEN ANOLE
(Anolis carolinensis)

DISTRIBUTION: Southeastern United States.

LENGTH: 6-8".

DESCRIPTION: A small, lively lizard often called a "chameleon." Although it can change color to a limited degree, the green anole cannot match the ability of the true chameleons in this respect. These lizards are probably the most commonly kept reptiles in the United States. The head is long with a pointed snout and there is a large distended dewlap, pink in color with white spots, in the male. The toes bear specially formed pads similar to those of the geckos that permit climbing of vertical surfaces, even glass, so an anole's cage should always be covered to prevent escape. The tail is long and easily broken. It regenerates quickly, but the regrown portion is incapable of color changes. The colors range from chocolate brown to ashy gray, olive-yellow, or bright green; the belly is white. Basks frequently. These reptiles are strictly arboreal.

HABITAT: Found throughout the southeastern United States; very common in most areas. Prefer the lower branches of trees and bushes. Frequently found in residential gardens and greenhouses.

CAGE: Woodland.

TEMPERATURE RANGE: 75-85°F.

FOOD AND WATER: The main diet consists of small insects and spiders. Supply a water dish for bathing. Anoles prefer to lap drops of water from the leaves of plants rather than drinking from a dish, so spray their cages daily. Drip system helpful.

SPECIAL NEEDS: Sunlight essential. Vitamins and bone meal should be added to food periodically.

YOUNG: Egg-layers, prefer moist soil or humus for laying, usually beneath a tree or bush. Young 2-3″ at hatching.

RELATED SPECIES: Similar to knight anole but much smaller.

KNIGHT ANOLE
(Anolis equestris)

DISTRIBUTION: Cuba; introduced into Florida.

LENGTH: 12-18″; average 14″.

DESCRIPTION: One of the largest anoles, the knight anole is a stately animal with a large head and huge pink dewlap. The toe pads are well developed, and these lizards are excellent climbers. The tail is long and fragile. These anoles do not have the green anole's color-changing ability. The body is bright green with yellow and white stripes and bars; the belly is white. There is a white stripe from the eye to the ear opening and another on the shoulder. There is a small dorsal crest behind the head; this head crest is usually raised when the dewlap is extended. These large lizards have been successfully introduced into several areas in Florida and have established breeding colonies.

HABITAT: The tops of large trees are the preferred habitat where the lizards can bask frequently. They rarely venture to the ground except for egg-laying.

CAGE: Woodland/rain-forest.

TEMPERATURE RANGE: 80-90°F.

FOOD AND WATER: Large insects, small rodents, and birds, as well as smaller lizards, make up the diet. A water pan should be provided for bathing, but these lizards will only drink drops of water from leaves. The cage should be sprayed daily.

SPECIAL NEEDS: Sunlight is mandatory. Vitamins and bone meal may be added to food as needed.

YOUNG: Egg-layers, prefer moist soil or humus for laying. Young 3-4″ at hatching.

RELATED SPECIES: Green anole is similar but much smaller. There are dozens of other anole species in tropical America, and several have been introduced into Florida.

COLLARED LIZARD
(Crotaphytus collaris)

DISTRIBUTION: Western North America.

LENGTH: 10-14″.

DESCRIPTION: Collared lizards are big-headed, long-tailed lizards of the American West. They are known in some areas as the "mountain boomer" and are the state lizard of Oklahoma. The neck is quite thin and is always marked with two broad black collars. The body coloration varies among the different subspecies and among males and females of the same subspecies. As a general rule, males are some shade of green, ranging from muddy olive to bright blue-green, with white spots on the back and a light brown to bright yellow head. The belly is greenish or dirty white. Females are usually dull brown with white spots and occasional salmon markings. The tail is extremely strong and, although it is detachable, a hard pull is required to remove it. Collared lizards are noted for their ability to run on the hind legs, resembling a miniature *Tyrannosaurus rex*. These lizards also have an interesting habit of waving the tail, much in the fashion of a cat, before lunging at prey. They bite hard when first captured but tame quickly and are quite long-lived.

HABITAT: Usually found in rocky, brushy areas; a favorite haunt is along dry creek beds. Occasionally venture into the yards of houses where insect food is abundant. The author had several living in and on a stone wall in his back yard in northeastern Oklahoma. Bask constantly.

CAGE: The best cage is a woodland cage without the woods. In other words, simply a large cage consisting of sandy soil, a few rocks, and a few low plants. A hiding place should be provided.

TEMPERATURE RANGE: 80-90 °F.

FOOD AND WATER: Insects, spiders, and small vertebrates are readily taken by most captives. Each individual will have its own preference. A small dish of drinking water should be provided.

SPECIAL NEEDS: Sunlight mandatory. Vitamins and bone meal should be added to food periodically.

YOUNG: Egg-layers, prefer sandy soil beneath a rock or bush for laying. Young 3-4″ at hatching.

RELATED SPECIES: Leopard lizard is quite similar.

LEOPARD LIZARD
(Gambelia wislizenii)

DISTRIBUTION: Western North America.

LENGTH: 12-15″.

DESCRIPTION: The leopard lizard is a large, big-headed, long-tailed lizard of the desert Southwest. Although basically similar in appearance to the collared lizard, the head is proportionately smaller. The ground color is beige or white with a profusion of brown or nearly black spots and bars. Occasionally flecks of red or orange are also present. The belly is usually white. The tail is strong but will detach. Leopard lizards share with collared lizards the habit of running on the hind legs, and these lizards will also wave the tail before attacking their prey. These animals are extremely voracious and often choke to death on animals which are too large to swallow. They bite hard when captured, but most individuals will tame in time.

HABITAT: Hot, arid regions that afford plenty of running room. While the collared lizard prefers rocky terrain, the leopard lizard will be found in flat, open areas. Bask constantly.

CAGE: Either a desert cage or one like that described for the collared lizard is satisfactory.

TEMPERATURE RANGE: 85-95°F.

FOOD AND WATER: Insects, spiders, and small vertebrates (especially small lizards) are readily accepted. Some flowers and buds may also be eaten. A small dish of drinking water should be supplied.

SPECIAL NEEDS: Sunlight mandatory. Vitamins and bone meal are very helpful.

YOUNG: Egg-layers, prefer sandy soil for laying. Young 3½-4".

RELATED SPECIES: Collared lizards are similar.

HORNED LIZARDS
(Phrynosoma spp.)

DISTRIBUTION: North America and Mexico.

LENGTH: 4-9".

DESCRIPTION: These are the "horny toads" of the Southwest. Horned lizards are stout, flat-bodied lizards with short, permanent tails. The body is covered with sharply spined scales on the back. The belly is white, smooth, and spineless. The heads of most species have a row of long sharp horns or spines sprouting from them, forming a protective collar. The ground color may be gray or brown with a scattering of dark blotches. Some white markings are also present, often outlining the dark spots. A few species vary from this general description, some having practically no spines at all and others having bright red, orange, or yellow patterns. Horned lizards are extremely docile animals, rarely attempting to bite. Most species run rather slowly and are easily caught by hand. When caught they may blow themselves up with air in order to appear more formidable. Also, when alarmed or annoyed some horned lizards have the disquieting habit of squirting droplets of blood from the eyes. They are fairly active during the day; at night they bury themselves in the desert sand.

HABITAT: Dry, rugged regions of the American Southwest. They are rarely found when you are looking for them exclusively, except in the most remote of areas. They normally just show up unexpectedly, sometimes venturing into the back yards of houses and even basking on patios.

Dorsal view of *Phrynosoma cornutum*, the horned lizard most often kept as a pet.

CAGE: Desert.

TEMPERATURE RANGE: 85-95 °F.; cannot digest food at temperatures lower than 70 °F. Dry heat is mandatory, and dampness can be fatal.

FOOD AND WATER: Ants are the natural diet. Other insects and invertebrates are readily accepted by most specimens but do not seem to be a satisfactory substitute for the ants. A small dish of water should be supplied and the lizards should be misted occasionally.

SPECIAL NEEDS: Sunlight is mandatory.

YOUNG: Egg-layers, prefer sandy soil for laying. Young 1-1½" at hatching.

RELATED SPECIES: Moloch is similar.

63

SAND LIZARDS, EARLESS LIZARDS
(*Holbrookia* spp.)

DISTRIBUTION: Southwestern North America.

LENGTH: 4-6".

DESCRIPTION: The sand lizards or earless lizards are a group of small, brightly colored reptiles common in coastal areas. The tail is fairly short and is easily broken. The body scales are smooth to the touch but bear minute keels. The nose is upturned and somewhat hooked for digging in loose sand. Specialized scales on the nose are formed into comb-like structures which keep sand out of the nostrils. These lizards have no external ear openings. The body color varies with geographical regions. Those specimens near the coast will have a light tan or gray dorsal surface. Those found further inland will be brown or dark gray. All males will have one or two black bars on the side of the body and most are washed with vivid yellow or orange on the sides and belly as well. The females lack the dark bars in most species but may still have the bright colors. These lizards are extremely agile and quick and often freeze in place or bury themselves in the sand in order to confuse a would-be captor or predator and escape.

HABITAT: Open sandy areas in the Southwest, particularly abundant in the sand dunes along the Texas coast. Bask frequently.

CAGE: Desert.

TEMPERATURE RANGE: 65-85°F.; very tolerant of temperature fluctuations.

FOOD AND WATER: Tiny insects, spiders, and sand fleas (amphipods) are the natural diet. I have also observed several specimens nibbling on sea oats and other dune plants. Do not attempt to keep these lizards unless you have access to a large supply of baby crickets or fruit flies. A small water dish should be supplied; add a bit of salt for coastal specimens.

SPECIAL NEEDS: Sunlight mandatory. Feed the crickets or flies a highly nutritious diet.

YOUNG: Egg-layers, prefer sandy soil for laying. Young ¾-1" at hatching.

64

In many lizards the dorsal coloration is very variable, as shown by these three *Uta stansburiana* from near Los Angeles. Photo by K. Lucas, Steinhart Aquarium.

RELATED SPECIES: Some of the fence swifts are similar in appearance, as is the side-blotched lizard.

SIDE-BLOTCHED LIZARD
(Uta stansburiana)

DISTRIBUTION: Western North America.
LENGTH: 4-6".
DESCRIPTION: Small agile lizards with short tails and occupying a variety of habitats, the side-blotched lizards are an important food item in the diets of many western animals, yet are interesting in habits and in many subspecies are quite brightly

65

colored as well. The tail is easily detachable as the lizard has no other defense except flight. The ground color may be brown or gray with a series of dark mottlings or bars across the back. The belly is dirty white. One subspecies has bright red, orange, yellow, and blue markings on the back and sides. All have a dark blotch on the side behind the front limbs. These lizards spend a great deal of time basking and scampering over rocks in search of food. Utas are excellent food lizards for larger species.

HABITAT: May be found in a variety of dry, warm areas from deserts to grasslands. Often found beneath stones or in rock crevices, avoiding the midday heat.

CAGE: Desert with an abundance of sturdy rocks.

TEMPERATURE RANGE: 80-95°F.

FOOD AND WATER: Small insects and other invertebrates are the natural diet. A small dish of drinking water should be supplied.

SPECIAL NEEDS: Sunlight mandatory. Food should be dusted with bone meal occasionally.

YOUNG: Egg-layers, prefer sandy soil for laying. Young 1-1½" at hatching.

RELATED SPECIES: Some varieties of the fence swifts and the sand lizards are similar.

CURLY-TAILED LIZARDS
(*Leiocephalus* spp.)

DISTRIBUTION: West Indies; introduced into Florida Keys.

LENGTH: Common curly-tailed lizard (*Leiocephalus carinatus*) 12-14"; red curly-tailed lizard (*Leiocephalus schreibersii*) 6-8".

DESCRIPTION: There are several species of curly-tailed lizards, of which the two mentioned above are the most commonly imported. The common curly-tail is a brown animal with light spots and striping and a short dorsal crest that continues well down the tail. It would tend to pass unnoticed if it were not for the unique habit of carrying the tail curled high over the back. The red curly-tail is similar but much more richly col-

Many species of curly-tailed lizards occur in the Caribbean islands. This is *Leiocephalus cubensis* from Cuba, a species seldom seen on the U.S. market. Photo by G. Marcuse.

Two large western American desert iguanids. Above, *Dipsosaurus dorsalis,* the desert iguana; below, *Sauromalus obesus,* one of several species of chuckwalla. Photos by K. Lucas, Steinhart Aquarium.

The two common water dragons. Above, *Physignathus cocincinus;* below, *Physignathus lesueurii.* Photos by G. Marcuse.

ored. The body is bright red with scattered turquoise spots, the legs are bright green with turquoise beneath, the tail is reddish brown and the head is black with white markings forming a raccoon-like mask. The red curly-tail cannot curl its tail as dramatically as the common curly-tail. All these lizards are alert, nervous, and quite curious reptiles that adapt easily to captivity and even thrive under conditions which would quickly kill many other lizards.

HABITAT: The common curly-tail prefers areas which permit climbing, such as rocky cliffs or sparse woods. The red curly-tail prefers flat arid regions with scattered rocks for climbing and basking. Often found on beaches.

CAGE: Woodland for the common curly-tail; desert for the red curly-tail.

TEMPERATURE RANGE: 80-90°F.

FOOD AND WATER: Insects, spiders, and other invertebrates are the usual diet. Larger specimens may be able to overcome small lizards or rodents. A small dish of water should be supplied for the red curly-tail. A small pan of water and a drip system should be supplied for the common curly-tail.

SPECIAL NEEDS: Sunlight mandatory. Occasional vitamin supplements may be needed for the red curly-tail.

YOUNG: Egg-layers, prefer sandy soil for laying. Young 2-2½" at hatching.

RELATED SPECIES: There are several species of curly-tails. Certain small agamids have the tail-curling ability but are seldom seen in captivity.

Agamidae

The Agamas

The agamas are the Old World counterparts of the iguanas. The only place in the world where iguanas and agamas coexist is the Fiji Islands group in the Pacific Ocean. The agamas vary in external appearance as greatly as do the iguanas.

Dorsal crests and dewlaps are especially prevalent, as is the color-changing ability. Most agamas have large heads, long tails, and powerful legs. The tongue is short, thick, and fleshy. The toes are usually heavily clawed for digging or climbing. Some aquatic species possess a laterally compressed tail for swimming. Others have prehensile grasping tails. The tails cannot be broken and regenerated. The teeth of agamas are acrodont and are diversified for different functions, just as in mammals. There are no legless species among the agamas and comparatively few with reduced limbs. Eyesight is extremely acute. Most agamas are egg-layers.

MOUNTAIN DRAGONS
(*Acanthosaura* spp.)

DISTRIBUTION: Southeastern Asia, Malaya, Sumatra.
LENGTH: 10-12".
DESCRIPTION: The mountain dragons are without question my
favorite lizards. Three varieties are commonly imported. *A. armata* is a foot-long dragon varying in color from olive to bright green with dark spots on the sides. The throat is orange in the male, and lilac streaks may appear on the neck of some specimens. *A. crucigera* is a foot-long dragon basically gray-brown in color with darker spots on the sides. The dewlap is black and the underside dirty white. *A. lepidogaster* is a ten-inch dragon that is mainly gray-green in color with a few dark

spots on the sides. The throat is light gray, black in some individuals, and the belly is white. All species are able to change color to some degree. All species are frog-like in appearance with moderately long tails swollen at the base in males. The tail cannot be regenerated if broken. There is a dorsal crest of long spines in *A. armata* and *A. crucigera* and short spines in *A. lepidogaster*. All species have a spine on either side of the neck and a movable spine behind each eye. Mountain dragons have strongly clawed forefeet for digging.

HABITAT: Dense mountain jungles; usually found on the ground or in low bushes. Fairly secretive; rarely bask.

CAGE: Rain-forest with plenty of water.

TEMPERATURE RANGE: 70-80°F.

FOOD AND WATER: Natural diet consists of earthworms and grubs; however, other insects, especially crickets and grasshoppers, are readily accepted. Occasionally feed at night. A large pan of water and a drip system are essential.

SPECIAL NEEDS: Sunlight beneficial. Vitamin supplements and bone meal should be added to all food.

YOUNG: Egg-layers, prefer moist earth or peat well sheltered by rotting wood or bark for laying. Young 2-3″.

RELATED SPECIES: Tree dragons (*Gonocephalus* spp.) are similar in many ways and were once grouped with the mountain dragons. Helmeted iguanas (*Corytophanes* spp.) are similar in appearance and in habits.

TREE DRAGONS
(*Gonocephalus* spp.)

DISTRIBUTION: Southeastern Asia, Indonesia, New Guinea, Australia.

LENGTH: 10-24″.

DESCRIPTION: The tree dragons are a large group of agamids sharing many traits in common with the mountain dragons. The head is large, most species having a large nuchal crest that continues down the back. All species have a large distensible dewlap which occasionally is spined along the outer edge.

The legs are long and end in long-toed feet that are heavily clawed for clinging to trees. The tail is long and in some species bears a short crest. The mouth is large and in the large species is capable of inflicting a nasty bite. Coloration varies from species to species, but most are some shade of brown or green with lighter or darker spots, stripes, and mottlings. Some species are splashed with bright blue, red, or yellow markings as well. The tail is strong and will not regenerate if broken.

HABITAT: Normally live high in trees in the dense rain-forests of southeastern Asia and Australia. Because of this they are difficult to locate and capture. Occasionally found on the ground among the undergrowth. Bask occasionally.

CAGE: Rain-forest with plenty of cover and limbs for climbing.

TEMPERATURE RANGE: 80-90°F.

FOOD AND WATER: Insects, spiders, and small vertebrates are readily accepted by most specimens. Earthworms may also be taken. A large pan of water should be supplied along with a drip system. These lizards require high humidity.

SPECIAL NEEDS: Some sunlight is beneficial. Vitamin supplements and bone meal are mandatory.

YOUNG: Egg-layers, prefer moist earth or peat for laying, usually beneath the roots of trees. Young 3-6" at hatching.

RELATED SPECIES: Mountain dragons.

LESUEUR'S WATER DRAGON
(*Physignathus lesueurii*)

DISTRIBUTION: New Guinea, Australia.

LENGTH: 24-36".

DESCRIPTION: These lizards are among the largest of agamids and are well adapted to aquatic life. The tail is long, broad, and oar-like for propulsion in swimming. There is a dorsal crest that is most pronounced on the neck and tail. The legs are powerful, and this lizard normally runs on its hind legs when in a hurry. The feet are heavily clawed as these lizards are excellent climbers as well. The body color is olive-gray with white stripes. These stripes continue onto the tail to form a banding effect. The lips are white, as is the throat. However, in one subspecies the throat and anterior portion of the belly are bright red. There is a black stripe running from the eye down onto the neck.

HABITAT: Prefer jungle trees overhanging rivers or other bodies of water. Bask frequently on limbs and dive into the water when alarmed.

CAGE: Only a very large cage will provide the necessary space requirements for these large lizards. The terrarium should be divided equally between land and water. Several large branches should overhang the water portion for basking purposes. The water should be kept clean with a substratum filter arrangement and water plants should be grown in it. Water depth should be at least 8-10".

TEMPERATURE RANGE: Land 80-90°F.

FOOD AND WATER: Insects, spiders, rodents, birds, frogs, and smaller lizards are the natural diet. Some plant material should also be supplied.

SPECIAL NEEDS: Sunlight is essential. Vitamin supplements and bone meal should be added to food frequently.

YOUNG: Egg-layers, dig long tunnels in moist soil beneath trees or bushes for laying. Young 6-8" at hatching.

RELATED SPECIES: Chinese water dragon.

CHINESE WATER DRAGON
(*Physignathus cocincinus*)

DISTRIBUTION: Southeastern Asia.

LENGTH: 24-30".

DESCRIPTION: The Chinese water dragon is a large agamid vaguely reminiscent of the green iguana. There is a dorsal crest most pronounced on the neck and a high crest on the tail. The tail itself is broad and flattened for swimming. The legs are strongly muscled and bear claws. Chinese water dragons climb nimbly and, like Lesueur's water dragon, run on their hind legs. The adults are solid green or olive with broad black bands around the tail. The belly is dull olive. The young are strikingly colored: the body is bright emerald green with turquoise stripes on the neck and back, the tail is banded with black, the eyes are a bright canary yellow, and the belly is bright yellow-green.

HABITAT: Prefer jungle trees overhanging rivers or other bodies of water. Bask frequently on limbs and dive into the water when alarmed or disturbed.

CAGE: A large cage as described for the Lesueur's water dragon is suitable.

TEMPERATURE RANGE: Land 80-90°F.; water 75-80°F.

FOOD: Insects, spiders, frogs, smaller lizards, rodents, and nestling birds are all included in the diet. Will also consume some plant material.

SPECIAL NEEDS: Sunlight mandatory. Vitamins and bone meal should be added to all plant food.

YOUNG: Egg-layers, dig tunnels beneath trees for laying. Young 6-7" at hatching.

RELATED SPECIES: Lesueur's water dragon.

SAIL-FIN DRAGON
(Hydrosaurus amboinensis)

DISTRIBUTION: New Guinea, Indonesia.

LENGTH: 30-36".

DESCRIPTION: The sail-fin dragon or soa-soa is the largest member of the agamid family. This lizard is extremely powerful in build, the legs are heavily muscled, and the feet are strongly clawed. Even so, the sail-fin dragon is a slow runner and is easily caught on land. The snout is very long compared to most agamids. There is a tall crest on the neck continuing down the back as a large "sail" supported by outgrowths from the vertebrae. Near the hips the sail recedes and then develops into an even taller sail on the broad laterally flattened tail. The sail-fin dragons are excellent swimmers. The basic color is olive-brown, but some specimens show flashes of bright green or have black bands on the sides. Because of its slow movements and the fact that the natives of New Guinea hunt it for its flesh, the sail-fin dragon is being exterminated in many parts of its range.

HABITAT: Found near rivers in the dense rain-forests. Bask frequently on low limbs of trees overhanging the water. They are good climbers.

CAGE: Same as described for the Lesueur's water dragon.

TEMPERATURE RANGE: Land 80-90°F.; water 75-80°F.

FOOD: The tender leaves and fruits of plants form the basic diet. Occasionally insects and small animals may be taken.

SPECIAL NEEDS: Sunlight beneficial. Add vitamins and bone meal to all plant food.

YOUNG: Egg-layers, tunnel beneath the roots of trees for laying. Young 7-9″ at hatching.

RELATED SPECIES: None. Resemble the water dragons in habits and the basilisks in appearance.

FLYING DRAGONS
(*Draco* spp.)

DISTRIBUTION: India through southeastern Asia.

LENGTH: 6-12″.

DESCRIPTION: The flying dragons are the only modern lizards besides the flying geckos that have developed the ability to actually glide through the air. The last few ribs on each side of the body are movable and covered with a thin, brightly colored webbing of skin that is their "wings." When resting, the wings are usually folded against the body. These lizards are extremely delicate creatures with a long thin neck, frail body, and long tail that is somewhat flattened at the base. There are three dewlaps, one on either side of the chin and one extremely long one on the throat. The ground color is brownish gray and the belly is white. The wings, depending on the species, are red, orange, yellow, black, or blue with white or black spots or stripes.

HABITAT: Normally found high in jungle trees. They rarely descend to the ground except for egg-laying.

CAGE: Woodland/rain-forest with heavy cover.

Head of *Draco maculatus*, a flying dragon. Photo by the author.

TEMPERATURE RANGE: 80-90°F.

FOOD AND WATER: Ants are the natural diet, but fruit flies or baby crickets in sufficient numbers are acceptable substitutes. Water is lapped from leaves instead of taken from a dish, so spray the cage each day. A drip system is essential. Difficult to maintain in captivity.

SPECIAL NEEDS: Sunlight mandatory.

YOUNG: Egg-layers, prefer moist soil beneath a tree or bush for laying. Young 1½-2½″ at hatching.

RELATED SPECIES: None.

Agama agama, one of the many species of common agamas. Photo by Dr. O. Klee.

COMMON AGAMAS
(*Agama* spp.)

DISTRIBUTION: Asia Minor, North Africa, Asia.

LENGTH: 6-14″.

DESCRIPTION: There are over sixty species in the genus *Agama.* However, most are similar in habits and all are similar in shape. The body is broad and flattened with a long tail. The head is large and is connected to the body with a rather thin neck. The legs are strong and are built for fast running. Some species have strongly keeled or even spiny scales; others have smooth scales arranged in regular rows. The colors vary from species to species. Most are an inconspicuous brown or tan color with a brighter head. In the breeding season, males of many species develop magnificent colors: blue, red, and yellow predominate. Agamas are strongly territorial and normally live in large family groups. They are mainly terrestrial animals.

HABITAT: Agamas occupy a wide variety of habitats, from desert to the borders of forests. The majority inhabit rocky grasslands.

CAGE: Most do well in a cage as described for the collared lizard. However, if your specimens seem to be inactive try a desert setup and increase the heat.

TEMPERATURE RANGE: 75-85°F. for most species; 90-100°F. for desert species.

FOOD AND WATER: Insects and spiders are the main diet. Some species also eat some plant foods. A water dish should be supplied for drinking and bathing.

SPECIAL NEEDS: Sunlight mandatory. Vitamins and bone meal should be added to all plant food.

YOUNG: Egg-layers, prefer sandy soil for laying. Young 2-2½″ at hatching.

RELATED SPECIES: Similar in some respects to certain iguanids such as the fence swifts.

BLOODSUCKERS
(*Calotes* spp.)

DISTRIBUTION: India through southeastern Asia.

LENGTH: 12-18″.

DESCRIPTION: Bloodsuckers or calotes are extremely common lizards in their natural habitats. The head is large and the shoulders are rather massive and strong. The tail is long and thin, as are the strong legs. The body is laterally flattened. The back bears a dorsal crest beginning on the neck and ending just short of the tail. There is a distensible dewlap that may be brightly colored in some species. The ground color is usually reddish brown or gray-brown. Certain species differ in that the main color is bright green. The belly is white or gray. The name "bloodsucker" originated because many species are able to develop a bright red color in the head and neck region. Most bloodsuckers have excellent color-changing abilities. When excited, some species are capable of turning a bright turquoise blue. These lizards bask freqently.

HABITAT: Bloodsuckers are always found in jungle trees or bushes. They rarely descend to the ground. They are quite prevalent in gardens and parks in India.

CAGE: Rain-forest with plenty of cover.

TEMPERATURE RANGE: 75-85°F.

FOOD AND WATER: Insects, spiders, small rodents, and smaller lizards are the natural diet. A large pan of water should be supplied with a drip system.

SPECIAL NEEDS: Sunlight mandatory. Bone meal and vitamins should be dusted on all food.

YOUNG: Egg-layers, prefer moist soil beneath a tree or bush for laying. Young 3-4″ at hatching.

RELATED SPECIES: Resemble the tree dragons and mountain dragons in certain respects.

NOSE-HORNED DRAGON
(Ceratophora stoddartii)

DISTRIBUTION: Sri Lanka.

LENGTH: 8-10″.

DESCRIPTION: These small dragons are unique in several ways. The anterior portion of the body is covered with large overlapping leaf-like scales that decrease in size posteriorly. The body is slightly flattened laterally and is well adapted to an arboreal existence. However, this lizard descends to the ground to drink and feed. The tail is long and thin, slightly swollen at the base. The legs are long and thin with strongly clawed feet. The oddest feature of this lizard is the long horn on the snout made of spongy tissue and quite flexible. The ground color is olive-green on the sides, darker on the back. The head is brown with white lips and throat, and the nose horn is white as well. The tail is brown, the belly white or gray.

HABITAT: Prefers low trees or bushes in mountain forests. Sometimes found on the ground among the undergrowth. Rarely bask; fairly secretive.

CAGE: Rain-forest with a great deal of cover.

TEMPERATURE RANGE: 65-75°F.

FOOD AND WATER: Insects, spiders, and earthworms are the primary foods. A large pan of water should be supplied as well as a drip system.

SPECIAL NEEDS: Some sunlight is beneficial. Vitamins and bone meal should be added to the diet.

YOUNG: Egg-layers, prefer moist soil beneath a bush or tree for laying. Young 2-2½" at hatching.

RELATED SPECIES: None.

THORN-TAILED AGAMAS
(*Uromastyx* spp.)

DISTRIBUTION: North Africa east into Asia Minor.

LENGTH: 12-24".

DESCRIPTION: The thorny-tailed agamas are creatures of the desert. The body is flat and broad, the head is short, blunt, and almost turtle-like in appearance. The legs are short and heavily muscled, ending in large feet with powerful claws. Although these heat-loving lizards are rather slow-moving, they are capable of burrowing with remarkable speed and dexterity. The tail is short and armed with rings of sharp spiny scales. This tail is used for defense and as a storage area for fat. The color varies even among individuals of the same species. The usual ground color is some shade of brown. However, these lizards are capable of altering their colors to a great extent; they may become bright orange, yellow, red, or even green on occasion. The head is usually darker than the body.

HABITAT: Prefer desert areas where they dig long burrows in the sand. Each lizard digs its own burrow and lives alone except during the breeding season, when the male and female share a burrow. Bask fequently at the burrow entrance.

CAGE: Desert with at least six inches of sand for flooring material.

TEMPERATURE RANGE: 90-100°F.; absolutely dry heat mandatory.

FOOD AND WATER: Feed exclusively on the leaves, flowers, and fruits of desert plants, which supply all the moisture these

Details of the heads of two thorn-tailed agamas. Above, *Uromastyx acanthinurus;* below, *Uromastyx hardwickii.* Photos by G. Marcuse.

lizards are able to obtain in the wild. Most adapt easily to other vegetable food. Supply a small dish of drinking water.

SPECIAL NEEDS: Dry heat and sunlight mandatory. Vitamins and bone meal should be added to all plant foods.

YOUNG: Egg-layers, lay in long burrows in the sand. Young stay in burrow for several days after hatching. Young 2-3″ at hatching.

RELATED SPECIES: None. Resemble certain small iguanids.

FRILLED DRAGON
(*Chlamydosaurus kingii*)

DISTRIBUTION: Australia.

LENGTH: 24-36″; one exceptional specimen was reported at 60″.

DESCRIPTION: The frilled dragon has developed the most extraordinary defense mechanism of any lizard. There is an enormous frill of skin behind the head which is supported by cartilage. This frill may be expanded to form a circle measuring a foot across in large specimens, but normally the frill is folded back against the body. The legs are long and powerful, and these lizards normally run on their hind legs. The tail is very long and cannot be regenerated if broken. The ground color is brownish gray with subtle rust or yellow shadings. The frill is brightly colored with black, yellow, red, brown, and white. These lizards bask frequently on low limbs of trees.

HABITAT: Prefers trees on the outskirts of forests. Occasionally descends to the ground to forage for food.

CAGE: Woodland.

TEMPERATURE RANGE: 80-90 °F.

FOOD AND WATER: Insects, spiders, smaller lizards, and rodents are the natural diet. Some plant material may also be taken at infrequent intervals. A large pan of water should be supplied. Drip system beneficial.

SPECIAL NEEDS: Sunlight mandatory. Some bone meal and vitamin supplements may be beneficial.

YOUNG: Egg-layers, prefer sandy soil for laying. Young 5-6″ at hatching.

RELATED SPECIES: None.

MOLOCH
(Moloch horridus)

DISTRIBUTION: Australia.

LENGTH: 10-12".

DESCRIPTION: The moloch is one of the most bizarre lizards. The snout is short and the head itself is rather small. There are large spines on the head, the two largest behind the eyes. There is a strange hump on the neck which seems to be a reservoir for fat and water storage. This hump is also studded with spines. The body is rather bulky and although the legs are fairly long and well-muscled, the moloch rarely moves at a pace faster than a slow walk. The body and legs are covered with spines, as is the short thick tail. The color pattern varies with geographical ranges. The main colors are rust, yellow, black, and brown in a striped or barred configuration.

HABITAT: Occupies the hottest, most arid areas in the Australian outback. They are well camouflaged against the red and yellow sands of the area, and the body colors combined with slow movements often make them difficult to see.

CAGE: Desert.

TEMPERATURE RANGE: 85-90°F.

FOOD AND WATER: Ants are the natural diet and no other insects seem to be a satisfactory substitute. Hundreds of ants may be consumed in a single meal, so molochs are difficult to maintain in captivity. Supply a small dish of water. It was once thought that these lizards absorbed water through the skin. Upon closer inspection minute canals were discovered between the scales which collect moisture and channel it to the mouth.

SPECIAL NEEDS: Sunlight and dry heat mandatory.

YOUNG: Egg-layers, lay in shallow burrows which they dig in the desert sand. Young 3-4" at hatching.

RELATED SPECIES: None. The horned lizards are similar in appearance.

Varanidae

The Monitors

Monitors include among their number the largest and heaviest lizards on earth. All monitors are the same shape but vary greatly in size. Monitors are long-lived for lizards, some having lived over 20 years in captivity. They are extremely responsive to gentle treatment and seem to be quite intelligent, most becoming tame in a short time as long as they are handled frequently.

The sense of smell is highly developed in monitors, the tongues being long and forked. The teeth are numerous and sharp. The neck is long and in some species bears a hump. The legs are long and powerful, and the toes have long sharp claws for climbing, digging, and tearing prey. The throat bears a large distensible pouch.

Unusual nape scalation of *Varanus rudicollis*, the rough-necked monitor. Photo by K. Lucas, Steinhart Aquarium.

The tail is long and is used for several purposes. First, as a weapon; damaging blows may be dealt with the tail of a large individual. Second, as a prehensile organ for climbing. Third, as an oar for swimming. All monitors are quite capable swimmers, and in semi-aquatic species the tail may be laterally flattened and ridged. The tail cannot be regrown if broken. Monitors have several traits in common with snakes, the most obvious being the ability to disengage the lower jaw from the skull in order to swallow large prey whole. Monitors are egg-layers.

NILE MONITOR
(Varanus niloticus)

DISTRIBUTION: Nile Valley and all subsaharan Africa.

LENGTH: 48-72"; average 60".

DESCRIPTION: The Nile monitor is one of the six largest monitors, with some individuals *said* to reach eight feet in length. As in all monitors the snout is long and the head is supported by a snake-like neck. The nostrils are placed high on the snout near the eyes, indicating an aquatic existence. The body is of slender build, except in older specimens, and the legs are long and powerfully muscled with the feet heavily clawed for digging. The tail is long, broad, and laterally flattened for swimming. It is also used as a powerful weapon. The ground color is blue-black or green-black broken with transverse stripes of yellow across the back made up of individual spots. There is a black stripe through and behind the eye, the tail is banded with black and yellow, and the throat and belly are yellow spotted with black. Nile monitors, though markedly aquatic animals, are fast runners and climb with ease.

HABITAT: Normally found along sluggish rivers and streams, digging in the silt for food. Often sleep in the water. These monitors can remain submerged for long periods. Young specimens sometimes bask on low limbs overhanging the water.

CAGE: Cage as described for the water dragon is suitable.

TEMPERATURE RANGE: 75-85 °F. land; 78-90 °F. water.

FOOD AND WATER: Nile monitors eat virtually any kind of animal material, dead or alive. In the wild they feed on frogs, molluscs, fish, water rats, and, oddly enough, the eggs and young of the Nile crocodile *(Crocodylus niloticus).* In captivity they will eat insects, earthworms, mice, rats, smaller lizards, and fish.

SPECIAL NEEDS: Sunlight mandatory. Add some vitamins and bone meal to the food periodically.

YOUNG: Egg-layers, prefer laying in termite mounds in the wild. Will lay in moist, well-sheltered soil in captivity. Young 8-10" at hatching.

RELATED SPECIES: All monitors are similar in appearance. The Nile monitor is easily confused with the water monitor.

WATER MONITOR
(Varanus salvator)

DISTRIBUTION: Southeastern Asia, Indonesia, Sumatra, Borneo.

LENGTH: 84-108".

DESCRIPTION: The water monitor is extremely common over most of its range, large specimens in particular being found. It is one of the three largest monitors. The snout is long and pointed and the neck is long and powerful. The nostrils are located on the end of the snout, one of the features that distinguish it from the Nile monitor. The tail is long, broad, and flattened laterally. The legs are long and powerful, ending in feet armed with sharp claws. These claws, the sharp teeth, and the powerful tail make a large individual a formidable opponent. In captivity, however, these large lizards become very docile. The color is blue-black broken with yellow stripes made up of individual spots or rosettes. There is a black stripe through and behind the eye, the throat is dirty white, the tail is banded with black and yellow, and the belly is white or gray.

HABITAT: Lives in heavily forested areas along watercourses where food is plentiful. Smaller specimens may climb into low

Head shape, nostril position, and scalation vary greatly in the monitors. Compare the green tree monitor, *Varanus prasinus,* above with the Komodo dragon, *Varanus komodoensis,* below. Photo above by G. Marcuse; that below by Dr. O. Klee.

The spotted tree monitor, *Varanus timorensis,* a species from Timor,
New Guinea, and northern Australia. Photo by Dr. O. Klee.

branches of trees to escape predators or to bask. Even large specimens may rest in trees.

CAGE: Cage for water dragons is suitable.

TEMPERATURE RANGE: 80-90°F. land; 78-90°F. water.

FOOD: Eats molluscs, frogs, insects, birds, rodents, fish, and smaller reptiles.

SPECIAL NEEDS: Sunlight mandatory. Add vitamins and bone meal to all food.

YOUNG: Egg-layers, prefer holes in trees or beneath tree roots for laying. Young 8-10″ at hatching.

RELATED SPECIES: Nile monitor is very similar.

CROCODILE MONITOR
(Varanus salvadorii)

DISTRIBUTION: New Guinea.

LENGTH: 72-108(?)″.

DESCRIPTION: The crocodile or Papuan monitor is a large lizard that has been said to reach 10 or even 12 feet in length. These reports are at best questionable, however. This large reptile is rare in the wild, or at least infrequent sightings would seem to indicate this. The crocodile monitor is a creature of the trees that descends to the ground to drink, breed, and occasionally to feed. The tail is extremely long and is used as a powerful weapon. The body is long and lithe, the limbs are strong, and the feet are heavily clawed. The neck is long and supports an unusual head that ends in a large bulbous snout that is unique among the monitors. The color is olive-brown to dark black-brown with yellow spots forming bands across the back and tail.

HABITAT: Lives in jungle trees in the tropical rain-forests of New Guinea. Not as dependent on water as are the Nile and water monitors.

CAGE: Large rain-forest.

TEMPERATURE RANGE: 80-90°F.

FOOD AND WATER: Rodents, birds, smaller reptiles, eggs, and insects make up the ideal diet. Supply a large pan of water equipped with a drip system.

SPECIAL NEEDS: Sunlight mandatory. Vitamins and bone meal should be added to all food.

YOUNG: Egg-layers, prefer hollow trees or burrows beneath the roots of trees for laying. Young 8-10″ at hatching.

RELATED SPECIES: All monitors are similar in overall shape, but none have the characteristic snout of the crocodile monitor.

GREEN TREE MONITOR
(Varanus prasinus)

DISTRIBUTION: New Guinea.

LENGTH: 36-48″.

DESCRIPTION: This is by far the most beautifully colored of all monitors. It has become fairly rare and as a result is rather high priced. This lizard is very slender and is arboreal in its habits. The tail is very long and thin and is prehensile. The body is elongated, as are the legs, and the toes are strongly clawed. The neck is long and slender with a pointed snout. The color is bright grass-green including the throat and belly, with thin black bands running down each side of the back. The eye is bright red in some individuals but usually is a coppery brown. This lizard spends most of its time in the trees but will descend to breed, drink, and forage for food.

HABITAT: Lives in trees in the tropical rain-forests of New Guinea. Rarely basks; prefers living in the lower branches under the shade of the high forest canopy.

CAGE: Rain-forest with thick cover.

TEMPERATURE RANGE: 80-85°F.

FOOD AND WATER: Feeds on birds and their eggs, smaller lizards, rodents, and insects. Supply a large pan of water equipped with a drip system. The environment in the cage must be fairly humid.

SPECIAL NEEDS: Some sunlight is probably beneficial. Add vitamins and bone meal to all food.

YOUNG: Egg-layers; lay in holes under the roots of trees. Young 7-9″ at hatching.

RELATED SPECIES: All monitors have the same general shape but none has the distinct coloration of the green tree monitor.

SAVANNAH MONITOR
(Varanus exanthematicus)

DISTRIBUTION: Africa south of the Sahara.

LENGTH: 48-60".

DESCRIPTION: The savannah monitor is probably the most commonly kept monitor due to its usually docile temperament and its ready availability. It is not a particularly unusual animal nor is it brightly colored, but it is extremely easy to care for. The body is rather stocky and the legs are fairly short and thickly muscled. The snout is blunt and the neck is shorter and thicker than in the four monitors discussed earlier. The tail is long and powerful with rough scales ringing the base. The color is a dark gray or dark brown; most specimens are unmarked but a few have light stripes or mottlings on the back. This desert dweller is strictly terrestrial in its habits.

HABITAT: Prefers hot, arid areas in subsaharan Africa. Basks frequently on rocks.

CAGE: Desert.

TEMPERATURE RANGE: 85-90°F.; absolutely dry heat mandatory.

FOOD AND WATER: Eats rodents, birds, insects, and smaller reptiles. A small dish of drinking water should be supplied.

SPECIAL NEEDS: Sunlight mandatory. With a varied diet, supplements are unnecessary.

YOUNG: Egg-layers, prefer burrows in sandy soil for laying.

RELATED SPECIES: All monitors are similar in shape.

Scincidae

The Skinks

The skinks are a diverse group of lizards that maintain a fairly consistent body shape in all species, the exceptions being those species with much reduced limbs and the legless species. The majority have small heads, thick necks, long bodies, and long breakable tails.

The scales of most skinks are smooth and appear polished, in some cases even iridescent. There is a great diversity in the tongues of these lizards. Most are short and fleshy with a slight notch at the end, but some species have large, flat, bright blue tongues. The dentition is pleurodont. Some skinks vary from the smooth scalation and have plate-like outgrowths of the body and tail and helmet-like protrusions on the back of the skull. One species has a short fat tail that is used as a decoy, while others have short, spiny tails used as weapons or long prehensile tails used for climbing. The sense of smell is excellent, as is eyesight, in most skinks. Some burrowing species have developed eyelids that are fused and have a transparent scale on the lower lid to see through when the eye is closed; other non-burrowing species may have the same feature. Skinks are both egg-layers and live-bearers.

BLUE-TONGUE SKINKS
(*Tiliqua* spp.)

DISTRIBUTION: New Guinea, Australia.
LENGTH: 18-30".
DESCRIPTION: There are several species of blue-tongue skinks, of which the giant blue-tongue skink *(Tiliqua gigas)* and the Australian blue-tongue skink *(Tiliqua scincoides)* are the most commonly seen and kept in captivity. Both are large,

93

Detail of the head scalation and mouth of a blue-tongue skink, *Tiliqua*. Photo by J. Warham.

heavy-bodied lizards with short thick tails. The head is massive with large jowls. The legs are short and widely separated with tiny feet and small claws. They move in a slow waddle that is rather comical. The tongue is large, flat, and bright cobalt. The scales are smooth and shiny as in most skinks. The giant blue-tongue skink is light brown or gray with several dark brown crossbands on the back and tail. The head is larger and less pointed than the Australian blue-tongue skink. This animal is gray with dark blue-black or brown-black crossbands on the back and tail.

HABITAT: The giant blue-tongue skink and the Australian blue-tongue skink both live in open arid areas with a minimal amount of cover. They are strictly terrestrial and bask occasionally. These lizards become extremely tame in captivity.

CAGE: Cage as described for the collared lizard is suitable.

TEMPERATURE RANGE: 75-85 °F.

FOOD AND WATER: The main food is plant material, but these skinks will also accept mice, insects, smaller lizards, and snails. Supply a pan of drinking water. Drip system beneficial.

SPECIAL NEEDS: Sunlight beneficial. Add vitamins and bone meal to all plant food.

YOUNG: Live-bearers, two or three young born at a time.

RELATED SPECIES: There are several species of blue-tongue skinks that are all similar in appearance.

PINECONE SKINK
(Trachydosaurus rugosus)

DISTRIBUTION: Australia.

LENGTH: 16-22".

DESCRIPTION: The pinecone skink or bobtail is a unique animal and a favorite among reptile keepers. Several herpetologists consider this lizard to be in the genus *Tiliqua* along with the blue-tongue skinks because of several anatomical similarities and the common characteristic of the bright blue tongue. The body is long and stocky. The legs are short and stumpy and resemble those of the blue-tongues. The tail is large and covered with large overlapping scales that give it the appearance of a pinecone. The scales on the head and body are also large and bony. The head and tail resemble each other superficially, which seems to confuse attackers. The overall appearance of the lizard is that of three pinecones glued together. The color varies with geographical area and may be solid black, dark gray, or dark brown. In some areas of Australia the bobtails are patterned red, rust, black, brown, and white and are quite striking.

HABITAT: Lives in the desert-grassland areas of southwestern

Two common American skinks. Above, the brown skink, *Leiolopisma laterale;* below, the western skink, *Eumeces skiltonianus.* Photo above by the author; that below by K. Lucas, Steinhart Aquarium.

Opposite:
Pinecone skinks, *Trachydosaurus rugosus.* These lizards are also common-ly called bob tail skinks or two-headed skinks for obvious reasons. Photo by J. Warham.

97

Australia. Often burrows into the sand dunes of the area to cool off. Basks frequently. These lizards become very tame in captivity and seem to be quite intelligent and responsive to gentle handling and treatment.

CAGE: Cage as described for collared lizards is suitable.

TEMPERATURE RANGE: 80-90°F.

FOOD AND WATER: Eats a variety of plant material plus insects, earthworms, and snails. Supply a pan of drinking water.

SPECIAL NEEDS: Sunlight beneficial. Add vitamins and bone meal to all plant food.

YOUNG: Live-bearers, give birth to two or three young at a time.

RELATED SPECIES: None. Similar in several ways to the blue-tongue skinks.

FIVE-LINED SKINK
(Eumeces fasciatus)

DISTRIBUTION: Eastern North America.

LENGTH: 6-9", exceptionally 11".

DESCRIPTION: The five-lined skink is an extremely attractive lizard common in the wooded areas of the southeastern United States. The body is long and circular in cross section. The head is usually fairly small and somewhat triangular in shape, although old males tend to develop heavy jowls. The legs are powerful and widely spaced. The tail is long and very fragile. It may be regenerated if broken. The scales are smooth and glossy, making these lizards difficult to hold. The jaws are strong, and large specimens are capable of biting painfully. They tend to hang on after biting, but remove them gently to avoid breaking the teeth. The ground color is dark brown or black with five light yellow or white stripes running the length of the back. The stripes tend to fade with age, and the head of the breeding male becomes a bright red.

HABITAT: Prefer sheltered areas near woods. Very secretive, usually found beneath rocks or logs or beneath the bark of trees. Rarely bask. Burrow readily and rapidly. Sometimes climb into low branches of trees as well.

CAGE: Woodland. Enjoys some moisture so spray the cage daily.
TEMPERATURE RANGE: 70-85°F.
FOOD AND WATER: Insects, spiders, and other small invertebrates make up the diet. Supply a small shallow dish of drinking water.
SPECIAL NEEDS: Sunlight is beneficial. Feed the insects a high-calcium diet.
YOUNG: Egg-layers, lay in hollow logs or burrows beneath rocks or tree roots. The female coils around the eggs and broods them until they hatch. Young are black with yellow stripes and a bright blue tail. About 1½-2" at hatching.
RELATED SPECIES: Many North American skinks are similar, including the broad-headed skink.

BROAD-HEADED SKINK
(Eumeces laticeps)

DISTRIBUTION: Eastern North America.
LENGTH: 8-12".
DESCRIPTION: A large skink of the southeastern United States and the second largest skink in North America. The body is long and round in cross section, and the head is large with swollen jowls. The legs are widely separated and quite powerful; the claws are large and strong for climbing. The tail is moderately long and fragile; it will regenerate when broken. As in the five-lined skink, the scales are smooth and glossy. When young, these skinks are similar in appearance to the five-lined skinks, but the stripes disappear with age to form a solid olive ground color. The head is red-orange. These skinks can bite painfully and tend to hang on tenaciously.
HABITAT: Found in open woodlands, usually well up in trees where they forage for food. Bask frequently. Sometimes found under the bark of trees or under rotting wood or rocks on the ground.
CAGE: Woodland.
TEMPERATURE RANGE: 70-85°F.
FOOD AND WATER: Insects, spiders, smaller lizards and

snakes, and small rodents are the primary diet. Supply a small shallow dish of water.

SPECIAL NEEDS: Sunlight beneficial. Add vitamins and bone meal to all food.

YOUNG: Egg-layers, laying habits similar to those of the five-lined skink. Young 2-2½ " at hatching.

RELATED SPECIES: No other skink in the southeastern United States is as large as this skink, nor are any skinks as arboreal in its range.

BROWN SKINK OR GROUND SKINK
(Leiolopisma laterale)

DISTRIBUTION: Eastern North America.

LENGTH: 3-5".

DESCRIPTION: This is probably the most common lizard of the southeastern United States. It is found in nearly all wooded areas, where its small size and protective coloration make it populous and successful. The body is long, as is the tail, and the head is quite small. The lower eyelid bears a clear scale through which the lizard can see with the eyes closed. The legs are short and weak, but movement is aided by a snake-like action of the body and tail. The tail may be broken in an emergency and regenerated. The scales are smooth and glossy. The color is some shade of brown with a dark stripe down the back. The belly is white.

HABITAT: Prefers moist woods, sometimes found deep in forests where very little light reaches the ground. Live beneath rocks, leaves, and rotting wood. Never climbs. Can swim well and often escapes predators by hiding in shallow water.

CAGE: Woodland.

TEMPERATURE RANGE: 65-85°F.; very tolerant of temperature fluctuations.

FOOD AND WATER: Only very small insects and spiders are eaten. Baby crickets are ideal. Supply a small shallow dish of water. Drip system probably beneficial.

SPECIAL NEEDS: No sunlight necessary. Feed insects a high-calcium diet.

YOUNG: Egg-layers, prefer moist soil beneath rocks or rotting wood for laying. Young 1-1½" at hatching.

RELATED SPECIES: None in the United States.

COMMENTS: Usually called *Lygosoma laterale* or *Scincella laterale* in literature.

RAINBOW SKINKS
(*Riopa* and *Mabuya* spp.)

DISTRIBUTION: Africa and the Indo-Australian archipelago—*Riopa;* South America, Africa, and the Indo-Australian archipelago—*Mabuya.*

LENGTH: 8-14".

DESCRIPTION: These skink genera comprise nearly 80 species. They are grouped together here because several species of each genus are frequently imported under the name of "golden skinks" or "African blue-tails." *Riopa* species have a round body, moderately long tail, and short, powerfully built legs. *Mabuya* species have a more flattened body for hiding in rock crevices. The tail is proportionately longer than in *Riopa* and the legs are longer as well. Both genera have brightly colored species among their number. Most *Riopa* species are some shade of gold or reddish brown and most *Mabuya* species are some shade of dark brown or gold-brown. Some species have bright blue tails and highly polished scales that may be iridescent. The tails of both species are fragile and may be regenerated when broken.

HABITAT: Mabuya is normally found in woodlands or rain-forests, while *Riopa* is more likely to be encountered in grasslands or sparsely wooded areas. Neither genus climbs, but both will bask frequently.

CAGE: Woodland or rain-forest.

TEMPERATURE RANGE: 75-85°F.

FOOD AND WATER: Insects, spiders, and smaller species of lizards are the primary diet. Supply a small dish of drinking water.

SPECIAL NEEDS: Sunlight beneficial. Add vitamins and bone meal to food for the brightest colors.

YOUNG: Most species bear live young that are 2-2½" at hatching.

RELATED SPECIES: There are almost 30 species of *Riopa* and 50 species of *Mabuya.*

SPINY-TAILED SKINK
(Egernia cunninghamii)

DISTRIBUTION: Australia.

LENGTH: 12-18".

DESCRIPTION: These large skinks are very active lizards well adapted to the harsh rocky environment of the Australian outback. The body is long and flattened for hiding in rock crevices. The head is short and flat, covered with fairly smooth scales that continue down the back. The tail is short and covered with a series of heavily keeled scales arranged in rings. It is used to dissuade enemies from continuing an attack. The majority of specimens are a uniform dark brown or black in color. These skinks are extremely agile but rarely climb.

HABITAT: Live in hilly, rocky country in Australia. Bask frequently on rocks under which they also cool off and shelter. Related species live on the outskirts of forests and in grasslands.

CAGE: Desert with abundant sturdy rocks.

TEMPERATURE RANGE: 75-85°F.

FOOD AND WATER: Eat insects, spiders, and smaller lizards. They are said to eat some plant material as well. Supply a small dish of drinking water.

SPECIAL NEEDS: Sunlight mandatory. Add vitamins and bone meal to all food.

YOUNG: Live-bearers, young 3-4" at birth.

RELATED SPECIES: There are several species of *Egernia* in Australia, all of which are fairly similar in appearance.

Cordylidae

The Girdle-tails

The girdle-tails or cordylids are heavily armored lizards that include four-legged, two-legged, and legless species. The scales are large, bony, and strongly keeled or spined. The tail is moderately long and covered by rings of spiny scales as well; only the belly is somewhat unprotected.

The shape of the head is always triangular when viewed from above and in most species is quite large. The four-legged species possess strong limbs and long claws for climbing on the rocks and cliffs that they inhabit. The sense of smell is good and the eyesight is sharp. The eyes are large and the tongue is short and slightly notched. The tail is breakable, but a hard pull is required to remove it as it is the main weapon of these lizards; it may be regenerated if broken. The girdle-tails are both egg-layers and live-bearers.

SPOTTED GIRDLE-TAIL
(Cordylus warrenii depressus)

DISTRIBUTION: South Africa.
LENGTH: 10-12".
DESCRIPTION: This animal is one of my personal favorites. In the best of health, the spotted girdle-tail is a true show animal. The body is squat and thick with spines along the sides. The head is triangular with spines along the back edge. The legs are long and powerful with short spines on the outer edges. The tail is long and covered with rings of sharp spiny scales. It is used mainly as a weapon, but can be broken if necessary to escape a predator and later regenerated. The ground color is dark brown to nearly black with scattered white or yellowish

103

spots. The spines are edged in yellow. The belly is yellowish-white as are the undersides of the legs and tail. These lizards become extremely tame in captivity and will take food from the hand.

HABITAT: Lives in rocky areas near woods where they can seek shelter beneath stones or bushes. Bask frequently atop large rocks.

CAGE: Desert with large rocks stacked into small cliffs and a few small plants. Use blasting sand for flooring material.

TEMPERATURE RANGE: 70-85°F.

FOOD AND WATER: Eats insects, spiders, other small invertebrates, and smaller lizards. Supply a large pan of water and a drip system.

SPECIAL NEEDS: Sunlight mandatory. Add vitamins and bone meal to all food.

YOUNG: Live-bearers, young 2-3″ at birth.

RELATED SPECIES: All girdle-tails are similar, but none are strikingly marked.

ARMADILLO LIZARD
(Cordylus cataphractus)

DISTRIBUTION: South Africa.

LENGTH: 6-8″.

DESCRIPTION: The armadillo lizard is a slow-moving species with a unique defense behavior. The body is short, flat, and stout with short powerful legs. The head is triangular and the back edge is armed with spines. The body and legs are edged with spines and covered in heavy plate-like scales. The nostrils are set on tiny tube-like structures on the end of the snout. The tail is of medium length and is covered with rings of heavy spiny scales. The color is a rich golden brown with black on the snout and occasionally on the throat and feet. When confronted by a larger enemy the armadillo lizard grasps its tail in its mouth and rolls into a ball, presenting its attacker with an unpalatable meal of spines. These lizards are quite sociable and normally live in groups.

HABITAT: Found on rocky walls and cliffs where they sunbathe regularly and shelter in crevices.

CAGE: Desert with large rocks stacked into small cliffs. Use blasting sand for flooring material.

TEMPERATURE RANGE: 70-85°F.

FOOD AND WATER: Diet consists of insects, spiders, and other small invertebrates. Supply a large dish of drinking water.

SPECIAL NEEDS: Sunlight mandatory. Add vitamins and bone meal to all food.

YOUNG: Live-bearers, young 2-3" at birth.

RELATED SPECIES: All girdle-tails are basically similar but none have the bizarre defensive maneuver.

JONES' GIRDLE-TAIL
(Cordylus jonesii)

DISTRIBUTION: South Africa.

LENGTH: 4-6".

DESCRIPTION: The Jones' girdle-tail is one of the smallest of the *Cordylus* genus. It is a rather non-descript little lizard but it is so inexpensive and easy to keep that it is best included in this book. The head is vaguely triangular in shape with small nubs on the back edge where the spines of the larger species would be. The body is covered with large bony scales, as are the short, powerful legs. The tail is the same length as the body and is covered by rings of spiny scales. The body color is solid dark brown on the back. The lips, throat, and belly are white or light gray. The male may develop a rust color on the sides of the neck before breeding. These lizards are extremely skittish even when kept in captivity for a long time.

HABITAT: Found in dry rocky areas with plenty of crevices in which to hide. More secretive than most species of *Cordylus*. Bask frequently but will dive into the nearest hiding place at the slightest disturbance.

CAGE: Desert with rocks stacked into miniature cliffs. Use blasting sand for flooring material.

TEMPERATURE RANGE: 70-85°F.

FOOD AND WATER: Eats insects, spiders and other small invertebrates. Supply a small dish of drinking water.

SPECIAL NEEDS: Sunlight mandatory. Add vitamins and bone meal to all food.

YOUNG: Live-bearers, young 1-1½″ at birth.

RELATED SPECIES: Many cordylids are similar but most have some sort of markings on the ground color.

SUNGAZER
(Cordylus giganteus)

DISTRIBUTION: South Africa.

LENGTH: 12-15″.

DESCRIPTION: The sungazer is a stately animal and the largest of the girdle-tailed lizards. The head is large and triangular with large spines along the back edge, the neck long and spiny. The body is flattened dorsoventrally, squat and heavy, with spines along the sides. The legs are long and powerful with spines along the back edge. The tail is of medium length and covered with rings of sharp-spined scales and is used as a powerful weapon. It cannot be broken and regenerated as can

Cordylus giganteus, one of the most spiny and largest of the cordylid lizards. Photo by K. Lucas, Steinhart Aquarium.

the tails of other girdle-tails. The color is medium brown fading to gold on the sides. Occasional solid brown specimens are also found. Of all the girdle-tails, the sungazer is the only species that will not tame.

HABITAT: Lives in dry, rocky areas in South Africa, usually near the base of hills or mountain. Enjoys basking on high cliffs with the forepart of the body raised, hence the name.

CAGE: Desert with sturdy rocks stacked to form small cliffs. Use blasting sand for flooring material.

TEMPERATURE RANGE: 75-85°F.

FOOD AND WATER: Eats insects, spiders, other small invertebrates, lizards, and rodents. Some specimens will also accept plant material as well.

SPECIAL NEEDS: Sunlight mandatory. Vitamins and bone meal should be added to all food.

YOUNG: Live-bearers, young 3-4" at birth.

RELATED SPECIES: All girdle-tail lizards look fairly similar, but the sungazer is the largest and most spinose of the group.

CRAG LIZARDS
(*Pseudocordylus* spp.)

DISTRIBUTION: South Africa.

LENGTH: 10-12".

DESCRIPTION: The crag lizards or false girdle-tails are an interesting group of cordylids that are much less spiny than their true cordylid relatives. The species most commonly imported is *Pseudocordylus subviridis,* the orange crag lizard. The head is triangular in shape but lacks the spines of the true cordylids. The body is squat and flattened, with small regular scales becoming larger ventrally. The tail is covered with rings of bony scales that are spiny near the base of the tail. The color differs in the male and female. The male is colored a somber gray on the back, turning to bright orange-yellow on the sides of the body and beneath the legs. There is a black collar on the neck in most specimens and two rows of black spots down the back. The sides of the tail are colored with alternating bands of black and yellow or white. The throat is white with a vertical streak of black or gray down the center. The belly is orange-yellow or white depending on the subspecies. The female is gray dorsally, white ventrally. The collar, spots, and bands on the tail remain the same.

HABITAT: Found in rocky areas, often basking on inaccessible cliffs.

CAGE: Desert with rocks stacked into small cliffs. Use blasting sand for flooring material.

TEMPERATURE RANGE: 75-85°F.

FOOD AND WATER: Insects, spiders, other small invertebrates, lizards, and small rodents are the chief diet. Some plant material may also be taken. A large dish of drinking water should be supplied. Drip system beneficial.

SPECIAL NEEDS: Sunlight mandatory. Add vitamins and bone meal to all food.

YOUNG: Live-bearers, young 2-2½″ at birth.

RELATED SPECIES: There are several species of *Pseudocordylus,* all of which are similar. The true cordylids are also similar, but most are more spinose.

FLAT LIZARDS
(*Platysaurus* spp.)

DISTRIBUTION: South Africa.

LENGTH: 6-10″.

DESCRIPTION: Flat lizards are aptly named: their bodies are flattened to the point of absurdity, with the head and tail also flattened. The long legs stick almost straight out from the body. There are rings of keeled scales encircling the base of the tail, but elsewhere the scales are rather smooth. The claws are extremely sharp, and these lizards are well adapted for climbing all but the smoothest vertical surfaces. The flat lizards are extremely agile and quick and are difficult to recapture after an escape. The tail will regenerate if broken. The color patterns are sexually dimorphic. In most species the male is bright blue in the head and neck region, green on the body, and red posteriorly. Others are red anteriorly and yellow posteriorly with no blue or green present. Nearly all females are black or dark blue with several yellow or white stripes down the back. The throat is usually blue-black, as is the belly.

HABITAT: Lives in rocky areas, often near a body of water though they rarely swim. Bask on rock walls and cliffs. Quick to take refuge in a rock crevice at the slightest disturbance. Its defense is similar to that of the chuckwallas.

CAGE: Desert with rocks stacked to form small cliffs. Use blasting sand for flooring material.

TEMPERATURE RANGE: 75-85°F.

FOOD AND WATER: Eats insects, spiders, and other small invertebrates. Supply a pan of drinking water and a drip system.

SPECIAL NEEDS: Sunlight mandatory. Feed the insects a high-calcium diet.

YOUNG: Egg-layers, prefer rock crevices for laying. Young 2-3" at hatching.

RELATED SPECIES: There are several species of flat lizards, all of which are very similar.

PLATED LIZARDS
(*Gerrhosaurus* spp.)

DISTRIBUTION: South Africa.

LENGTH: 18-24".

DESCRIPTION: The plated lizards were once placed in a family of their own, the Gerrhosauridae, but anatomical similarities to the cordylids brought about their reclassification. These lizards are large thick-bodied animals with powerful legs built for both speed and digging. The tail is long and sturdy and, although it can be broken and regenerated, it is more commonly used as a weapon. It is thick at the base and covered in rings of heavy scales. The head is long and somewhat triangular in shape. Both head and body are covered with large plate-like scales, hence the common name. There is a long lateral fold on each side of the body. The usual coloration of most species is golden brown to dark brown above with a lighter gold throat and a dark brown to black belly. Some

Detail of the head of *Gerrhosaurus* sp. Notice the distinct lateral fold typical of the family Cordylidae. Photo by G. Marcuse.

species are more brightly colored with red and gold markings.

HABITAT: Prefer living on rocky hills with sparse vegetation. Hide in cracks in the rocks where they effect the defense posture of the chuckwallas. Bask frequently at the entrance to their burrows, which they dig beneath sheltering rocks.

CAGE: Cage as described for the collared lizard is ideal.

TEMPERATURE RANGE: 75-85°F.

FOOD AND WATER: Most species are omnivorous. Most will eat tender leaves and fruits as well as insects, spiders, and other small invertebrates. Larger individuals will eat small rodents, lizards, and birds. Supply a large pan of water for drinking and bathing.

SPECIAL NEEDS: Sunlight mandatory. Add vitamins and bone meal to all food.

YOUNG: Egg-layers, prefer laying in their burrows. Young 5-6″ at hatching.

RELATED SPECIES: There are several species of plated lizards, all of which are similar in appearance. The Madagascar plated lizard is also similar.

110

MADAGASCAR PLATED LIZARD
(Zonosaurus madagascariensis)

DISTRIBUTION: Madagascar.

LENGTH: 15-20".

DESCRIPTION: This large reptile is one of the most sought-after lizards in private collections. The body is flat and stout, covered with large horny plates. There is a lateral fold on each side of the body. The legs are strong and designed for digging and running. The tail is long and powerful. It may be regenerated if broken. The snout is pointed and the head is vaguely triangular in shape. The dorsal surface is black spotted with yellow or white. There is a yellow stripe on either side of the body beginning above the eye and ending at the base of tail. The belly is yellow and the throat is often bright orange in the male.

HABITAT: Lives along the banks of jungle rivers, where it digs burrows beneath the roots of trees overhanging the water. Bask occasionally.

CAGE: Rain-forest.

TEMPERATURE RANGE: 80-90°F.

FOOD AND WATER: Eats insects, small lizards, rodents, and some plant material as well. Supply a large pan of water for drinking and bathing and a drip system.

SPECIAL NEEDS: Sunlight beneficial. Add vitamins and bone meal to all plant food.

YOUNG: Egg-layers, lay in burrows under the roots of trees. Young 4-5" at hatching.

RELATED SPECIES: All three species of *Zonosaurus* are similar in appearance. The plated lizards are also very similar.

GIRDLED SNAKE-LIZARDS
(Chamaesaura spp.)

DISTRIBUTION: South Africa.

LENGTH: 18-24".

DESCRIPTION: The girdled snake-lizards are a unique group of cordylids with reduced limbs and a snake-like body. The head is long and pointed, and the body is elongated with widely spaced limbs. The legs are tiny, and in some species there are no front legs at all. The tail is whiplike and is usually two to three times the length of the body. It can be broken and regenerated if the lizard is attacked by a predator. The scales are large and plate-like with strong keels running down the middle. These lizards travel in an awkward undulating movement on the ground but are quite agile when moving through bushes or tall grass. The body feels brittle to the touch, without the suppleness and flexibility of snakes. The color varies from gray-brown to golden brown above, white below.

HABITAT: Found mainly in elevated grasslands with plenty of cover. Bask frequently but are skittish and quick to take flight.

CAGE: An enclosure such as that described for the collared lizard is satisfactory, but add a dried bush or two. Tumbleweeds are ideal.

TEMPERATURE RANGE: 75-85°F.

FOOD AND WATER: Feeds chiefly on insects in the wild, usually grasshoppers, crickets, and beetles. Supply a pan of water for drinking and bathing. Drip system may be beneficial. These lizards are difficult to maintain over long periods in captivity and I do not recommend them to the beginning herpetologist.

SPECIAL NEEDS: Sunlight beneficial. Add vitamins and bone meal to the diet of the insects you offer as food.

RELATED SPECIES: There are several species of girdled snake-lizards, all of which are very similar in appearance.

Gekkonidae

The Geckos

The geckos are unique and distinct from other lizards in many ways. First, they have possibly the widest range of tail variation among all the lizard families. The tail may be long and cylindrical, as in most lizards, or it may be short and knobby, flattened with gliding extensions, shaped like a leaf, shaped like a carrot, or short, fat, and pointed. Regardless of its shape, the tail may be regenerated if broken.

The skin of geckos is soft, flabby, and covered with small scales. The eyes in most species are lidless, being covered by a single transparent scale as in the snakes. The tongue is usually long and flat and is used to clean the eyes. Geckos have true voices, some being extremely loud. Most are nocturnal, and the eyes have vertical pupils. These pupils can be closed to form three or four small pinholes that admit light and focus sharply. Some geckos are notable exceptions to this rule, such as the Madagascar day gecko, which is diurnal and has round pupils. Most geckos possess special toe pads that allow them to cling to and climb vertical surfaces. The geckos are egg-layers.

Geckos are often found in close association with man, even entering houses to look for shelter or food.

TOKAY GECKO
(Gekko gecko)

DISTRIBUTION: Southeastern Asia.
LENGTH: 10-14".
DESCRIPTION: The tokay is one of the largest geckos. It has been spread world-wide by commerce and is probably the most commonly kept gecko in captivity. The head is large,

113

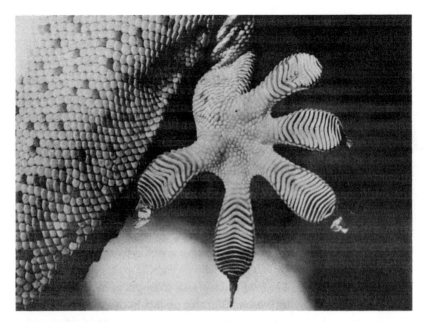

Detail ventral view of the foot of *Gekko gecko* showing the broad digits with lamellae below. Photo by G. Marcuse.

Ptychozoon kuhli, a flying gecko. Photo by K. Lucas, Steinhart Aquarium.

Above is *Pachydactylus bibroni,* Bibron's gecko. Photo by the author.

The leopard gecko, *Eublepharis macularius,* is a brightly colored Asian gecko with movable eyelids. Photo by K. Lucas, Steinhart Aquarium.

broad, and flattened, with a huge mouth. The body is flattened as well and is covered by tiny scales and soft skin. The legs are fairly long and end in extraordinary feet. The toes end in specialized pads that allow the lizard to climb vertical surfaces with ease and even run across ceilings. The eyes are covered with single clear scales that the lizard cleans with its tongue, as there are no movable eyelids. The voice is a loud scream, "GEK-KOH" or "TO-KAY." The color is light blue or gray with rust-colored spots. The belly is white. This gecko is strictly nocturnal. It will bite readily and hard.

HABITAT: Found near human dwellings, often inside houses. Also found in trees and on rock walls.

CAGE: Woodland. Tokays may also be released in the house if you have roaches or waterbugs. Only do this if the house has not been sprayed for insects. Usually hide behind picture frames during the day.

TEMPERATURE RANGE: 65-80°F.

FOOD AND WATER: Eats insects, spiders, lizards, small rodents, and anything else it can catch and swallow. Supply a small dish of drinking water.

SPECIAL NEEDS: Sunlight unnecessary. Add some bone meal and vitamins to food occasionally.

YOUNG: Egg-layers, lay on walls, in rock crevices, or under the eaves of houses. The eggs are sticky and adhere readily to almost any surface. Young 2-3" at hatching.

RELATED SPECIES: There are several geckos similar to the tokay, but none have the blue coloration.

MADAGASCAR DAY GECKO
(Phelsuma madagascariensis)

DISTRIBUTION: Madagascar.

LENGTH: 8-12".

DESCRIPTION: This is possibly the most beautifully colored of all lizards. These geckos are unusual in that they are strictly diurnal. The head is long, pointed, and slightly flattened. The body is rather plump and is somewhat flattened as well. The tail is cylindrical, heavy, and may be regenerated if broken. The legs are rather short, but these lizards can move very rapidly. The eyes are typically gecko, being covered with a single clear scale. The feet bear toe pads that allow these geckos to cling to vertical surfaces. The voice is a loud croak. These lizards can change color to some degree, but the usual color is a magnificent bright emerald green with several bright red streaks and spots on the head and back; the belly is greenish white.

HABITAT: Found on jungle trees in the rain-forests of Madagascar. Bask frequently.

CAGE: Rain-forest with plenty of branches and cover.

TEMPERATURE RANGE: 75-85°F.

FOOD AND WATER: Eats insects, spiders, and occasionally smaller lizards. May eat soft fruits and the nectar of flowers as well. Supply a pan of water for drinking and install a drip system. Spray the cage daily.

SPECIAL NEEDS: Sunlight beneficial. Add vitamins and bone meal to all food.

YOUNG: Egg-layers, eggs adhere to walls, rock crevices, or beneath bark of trees. Young 2-2½" at hatching.

RELATED SPECIES: There are several species of *Phelsuma,* all of which are colored similarly. This species is the largest, however.

BIBRON'S GECKO
(Pachydactylus bibroni)

DISTRIBUTION: South Africa.

LENGTH: 6-8".

DESCRIPTION: The Bibron's gecko is a commonly imported lizard that is extremely hardy in captivity. It is popular because it is often active during the day as well as at night. The head is broad and triangular in shape with clear scales covering the eyes. There are no movable eyelids. The body is short and stocky with four strong legs. The toes bear the typical gecko toe pads. The tail is short and fat and may be regenerated if broken. The scales are large and resemble warts. The color varies from gray-brown to dark brown. The warts are brown or light gray, forming a salt and pepper effect. There is a dark streak through the eye.

HABITAT: Usually found on or in trees or rock walls. Often venture near human dwellings. Prefer a temperate climate.

CAGE: Woodland with plenty of ground cover.

TEMPERATURE RANGE: 70-80°F.

FOOD AND WATER: Diet consists of insects, spiders, and other small invertebrates. Supply a dish of drinking water. Drip system is beneficial.

SPECIAL NEEDS: Sunlight unnecessary. Feed the insects a high-calcium diet.

YOUNG: Egg-layers, eggs adhere to rock crevices, beneath the bark of trees, or under logs. Young 2″ at hatching.

RELATED SPECIES: There are many geckos that are very similar in appearance, but most are smaller.

TURKISH GECKO
(Hemidactylus turcicus)

DISTRIBUTION: Originally the Mediterranean area; distributed world-wide by man.

LENGTH: 4-6″.

DESCRIPTION: The Turkish gecko is a true world traveler. Successful colonies have been established all over the world including the southeastern United States as a result of stowing away on commercial ships. The head is broad and rectangular, the eyes are covered by clear scales, and there are no movable eyelids. The body is short and stocky and is covered with warty scales. The legs are strong and end in toes bearing the typical gecko toe pads. The tail is of medium length and rather plump. The main color is light tan or gray-brown interspersed with darker warts. There is a dark streak through the eye. The belly is a dirty white color. These lizards are most active at night.

HABITAT: Found almost exclusively around human habitations or old deserted buildings. Prefers a temperate climate.

CAGE: Woodland with plenty of cover.

TEMPERATURE RANGE: 70-85°F.

FOOD AND WATER: Eats a wide variety of insects, spiders, and other small invertebrates. Can easily dispatch a full-grown cricket. Supply a small dish of drinking water.

SPECIAL NEEDS: Sunlight unnecessary. Feed the insects a highly nutritious diet.

YOUNG: Egg-layers, eggs will adhere to any surface, usually laid in a rock crevice or under the eaves of houses. Young 1½-2" at hatching.

RELATED SPECIES: There are many species of geckos that are similar. Most can be kept successfully as described above.

FLYING GECKOS
(*Ptychozoon* spp.)

DISTRIBUTION: Southeastern Asia including Indonesia.

LENGTH: 6-8".

DESCRIPTION: The flying geckos display yet another unique adaptation to a hostile environment among the lizards. The head, body, and tail are extremely flattened. The head is broad and bears loose flaps of skin along the sides, and the body is moderately long and has a fold of skin on either side that may measure ½" wide. The tail is long and has a ruffled appearance caused by additional loose folds of skin along the sides. When fleeing an attacker, these geckos will leap from their perch, stretch the folds of skin, and glide to the ground or to a lower branch. The folds act more as a parachute than as wings. The voice is a soft croak. The color is a gray-brown with darker bars and mottlings across the back.

HABITAT: Usually found on jungle trees where their irregular outline and subdued coloration blend with the bark. Active at dusk and at night.

CAGE: Rain-forest with plenty of branches and cover.

TEMPERATURE RANGE: 70-85°F.

FOOD AND WATER: Eat a variety of insects. In the wild the usual diet is termites, ants, and flies. Will readily accept crickets in captivity. Supply a small pan of water for drinking and a drip system. Spray the cage daily.

SPECIAL NEEDS: Sunlight unnecessary. Feed the insects a highly nutritious diet.

YOUNG: Egg-layers, eggs adhere to crevices in the trees or beneath the bark. Young 2-3" at hatching.

RELATED SPECIES: There are several species of flying geckos, all of which are similar.

LEAST GECKOS
(*Sphaerodactylus* spp.)

DISTRIBUTION: West Indies including the Florida Keys.

LENGTH: ¾-2½".

DESCRIPTION: The least geckos include among their number the smallest lizards in the world. The snout is long and pointed, and the eyes are covered with clear scales rather than movable eyelids. The back is covered with tiny scales and soft skin. The body is long and rather plump with four short, strong legs. The toes bear pads that enable these lizards to climb vertical surfaces. The tail is moderately long and plump. The voice is a barely audible squeak. Color varies with species, ranging from yellow to gray to green or brown, with the tail usually lighter in color than the body. There is also normally a profusion of tiny spots on the dorsal surface, dark on light-colored animals, light on dark animals. These geckos are active at dusk and at night.

HABITAT: Usually found in and around human habitations but also found on trees and bushes.

CAGE: Woodland with plenty of cover.

TEMPERATURE RANGE: 70-85°F.

FOOD AND WATER: Natural diet consists of tiny insects and spiders. Supply a small dish of drinking water and a drip system. Spray the cage daily.

SPECIAL NEEDS: Sunlight mandatory. Feed the insects a highly nutritious diet.

Coleonyx variegatus, the banded gecko. Juveniles (above) often have the bands more sharply defined than the adults, but there is much variation. Photo above by the American Museum of Natural History; that below by K. Lucas, Steinhart Aquarium.

YOUNG: Egg-layers, eggs adhere to whatever surface is chosen by the female. Young ½-¾" hatching.

RELATED SPECIES: There are about 60 species of least geckos, all of which are generally similar. Night lizards are also similar.

BANDED GECKO
(Coleonyx variegatus)

DISTRIBUTION: Southwestern North America.

LENGTH: 4-6".

DESCRIPTION: The banded gecko and relatives are unique among the geckos by being species possessing movable eyelids. The head is rather round with a short pointed snout. The neck is long and thin. The body is somewhat elongate with short widely spaced limbs. The toes bear no specialized pads as these lizards are terrestrial. The body is covered with tiny scales and soft, almost transparent skin. The tail is fairly long and is used as a reservoir for fat; it may be broken in an emergency and regenerated. The color is tan or yellow with brownish "saddles" across the dorsal surface; the belly is white. This gecko is strictly nocturnal. It's voice is a shrill squeak.

HABITAT: Lives among rocks in the arid desert Southwest. Usually found in sparsely vegetated areas. Never basks.

CAGE: Desert.

TEMPERATURE RANGE: 75-85°F.

FOOD AND WATER: Eats insects and spiders. Rarely drinks, but supply a small dish of water.

SPECIAL NEEDS: Sunlight unnecessary. Feed the insects a high-calcium diet.

YOUNG: Egg-layers, lay beneath rocks or in small sheltered holes.

RELATED SPECIES: The very similar reticulated gecko (*Coleonyx reticulatus*) and the Texas gecko (*Coleonyx brevis*) are the only native geckos with which the banded gecko could be confused.

Anguinidae

The Lateral-Fold Lizards

The lateral-fold lizards are a widespread group of lizards made up of both legless and four-legged forms. One minor group has two fin-like hind limbs resembling those of the flap-footed lizards. Another group, the alligator lizards, has a long lateral fold running the length of each side of the body.

Nearly all species are skink-like in appearance with smooth, polished scales. There are exceptions to this rule, however. All species have elongated bodies and long tapering tails that may be regenerated if broken. The legs are short but powerful and end in strong claws. The bodies of legless species feel rather stiff and brittle compared to the lithe, supple feel of snakes. Also, these lizards move rather awkwardly and without the fluid smoothness of snakes.

The teeth are flat and are used for grinding in most species, except for the slowworm. The tongue is long and slightly notched. There are no dorsal crests and dewlaps. The lateral-fold lizards are both egg-layers and live-bearers. All species become fairly tame in captivity, recognizing their keeper and accepting food from the hand. Most species are rather long-lived.

ALLIGATOR LIZARDS
(*Gerrhonotus* spp.)

DISTRIBUTION: Western North America through Central America.

LENGTH: 12-24".

DESCRIPTION: The alligator lizards are an interesting group of reptiles. The head is long and pointed in most species. The body is cylindrical and somewhat elongated with short legs

123

Two uncommon and unusual geckos. Above, *Hemitheconyx caudicinctus,* the fat-tailed gecko of western Africa; below, *Teratoscincus scincus,* the skink-like sand gecko of Asia. Photo above by K. Lucas, Steinhart Aquarium; that below by G. Marcuse.

Two very different anguinid lizards. Above, *Gerrhonotus multicarinatus,* an alligator lizard; below, *Ophisaurus apodus,* the sheltopusik. Photo above by K. Lucas, Steinhart Aquarium; that below by G. Marcuse.

that are widely separated, and the tail is long and prehensile. The dorsal scales are large and platelike, so when combined with the shape of the body these lizards do look like miniature alligators. The color varies with species, most being some shade of gray or brown with rust, black, and white markings. Some species are among the most beautifully marked of all lizards. These lizards are extremely agile and strong. Due to their size they are confident animals and rather slow and deliberate in their movements. Newly captured specimens may bite, but they tame quickly. They are very friendly and intelligent lizards.

HABITAT: Usually found in sheltered wooded areas. Most species are excellent climbers, and some may be found in the tops of trees. Bask occasionally but not habitually.

CAGE: Woodland with plenty of cover and branches.

TEMPERATURE RANGE: 70-80°F.

FOOD AND WATER: Eats insects, spiders, other small invertebrates, smaller lizards, small rodents, and eggs. Supply a pan of water for drinking and bathing. Drip system probably beneficial.

SPECIAL NEEDS: Sunlight beneficial. Add vitamins and bone meal to all food.

YOUNG: Species living in cooler climes are live-bearers, those living in warmer areas are egg-layers. Young 3-4″ at hatching.

RELATED SPECIES: There are many species of alligator lizards, all quite similar in appearance. The galliwasps are also similar.

AMERICAN GLASS LIZARDS
(*Ophisaurus* spp.)

DISTRIBUTION: North America, relatives found in Asia.

LENGTH: 24-42″.

DESCRIPTION: The American glass lizards are usually mistaken for snakes and killed by daring outdoorsmen. The snout is long and pointed, the tongue is long and forked and is protruded constantly, the eyes have movable eyelids, and there

Ophisaurus ventralis, the common glass lizard of the southeastern United States. Photo by the American Museum of Natural History.

are external ear openings. The body is long and snake-like with no external traces of legs; it feels brittle to the touch. The tail is extremely long and fragile; as expected, it may be regenerated when broken. The color varies with species; various shades of brown, gold, and green are the norm, some having black stripes or spots on the back. These lizards raise up like cobras when annoyed and puff out the throat. This threat is usually followed by a bite. While most tame down quickly in captivity, some maintain a nasty dispostion all their captive lives.

HABITAT: Found almost exclusively on the ground or in tall grasses near the edges of woods. Occasionally venture into low bushes to search for food. Burrow occasionally. Rarely bask.

CAGE: Cage as described for collared lizards is ideal.

TEMPERATURE RANGE: 75-85°F.

FOOD AND WATER: Eats insects, spiders, other small invertebrates, lizards, snakes, frogs, rodents, birds, and eggs. Supply a pan of water for soaking and drinking.

SPECIAL NEEDS: Sunlight beneficial. Add vitamins and bone meal to food occasionally.

YOUNG: Egg-layers, lay in burrows or hollow logs where the female coils around the eggs and broods them until they hatch. Young 5-6" at hatching.

RELATED SPECIES: There are three species of glass lizards found in the United States, with the main differences being the color pattern. Similar to the sheltopusik and the slowworms as well.

SHELTOPUSIK
(Ophisaurus apodus)

DISTRIBUTION: Asia Minor and western Asia.

LENGTH: 48-54".

DESCRIPTION: The sheltopusik is the largest of the lateral-fold lizards and the largest legless lizard. The head is rather blunt, with movable eyelids and external ear openings. The body is heavy, long, and snake-like with no external traces of limbs. The tail is extremely long and may be regenerated if broken. There is a lateral fold on each side of the body. The scales of the body are large and plate-like, arranged in rings around the body. The color is brown, gray, or rust above, yellow below. The sheltopusik is an active lizard that is strictly diurnal in habits. Since it tames quickly and is very long-lived, the sheltopusik is a common animal in reptile collections. It is very hardy in captivity.

HABITAT: Found in rocky meadows and thorny thickets in Asia Minor and western Asia. Strictly terrestrial. Basks frequently.

CAGE: Cage like that described for the collared lizard is ideal.

TEMPERATURE RANGE: 65-80°F.

FOOD AND WATER: Diet consists of snails, slugs, earthworms, insects, small lizards, and rodents. Supply a large pan of water for soaking and drinking.

SPECIAL NEEDS: Sunlight beneficial. Add vitamins and bone meal to all food.

YOUNG: Egg-layers, prefer sandy soil for laying. Young 6-8″ at hatching.

RELATED SPECIES: Similar to but longer and thicker than the slowworm and the American glass lizard.

SLOWWORM
(Anguis fragilis)

DISTRIBUTION: Europe, Asia Minor, western Asia, extreme northern Africa.

LENGTH: 12-18″.

DESCRIPTION: Slowworms are among the commonest of European reptiles, although many are killed each year, being mistaken for snakes. The snout is long and pointed. The body is long and snake-like with no visible limbs. The tail is two to three times the length of the body and is extremely fragile; it can regenerate when broken. The color varies as to subspecies, with brown, coppery red, and even black individuals common; black stripes may appear on the dorsal surface of some specimens. The young are silver. Slowworms are rather slow-moving creatures and are ideal lizards for observation in captivity as they tame quickly and are very long-lived.

HABITAT: Found in a variety of habitats from woodlands to grasslands. Strictly terrestrial. Bask occasionally. Dig burrows in which they retire during the heat of the day and at night.

CAGE: Woodland or one as described for the collared lizard is suitable. Use peat moss or soil for flooring material.

TEMPERATURE RANGE: 70-80°F.

FOOD AND WATER: Main diet is slugs and earthworms. Occasionally insects and smaller lizards are also taken. Supply a small pan of water for drinking.

SPECIAL NEEDS: Sunlight beneficial. Add vitamins and bone meal to food periodically.

YOUNG: Live-bearers, young 3-4″ at birth.

RELATED SPECIES: Similar to the sheltopusik and the American glass lizards but much smaller.

GALLIWASPS
(*Diploglossus* spp.)

DISTRIBUTION: Central and South America, West Indies.

LENGTH: 12-20".

DESCRIPTION: The galliwasps are unique lateral-fold lizards occasionally imported into the United States. They resemble the alligator lizards, but there are several obvious differences. The head is blunt but long and somewhat skink-like in appearance. The body is thick and cylindrical with small smooth scales. The legs are short and widely separated. The tail is of medium length and quite stout; if necessary it may be broken and regenerated in an emergency. The color scheme of some species is very striking, especially just after a shed. The ground color may be silver-gray with thin black stripes across the back and the belly a bright crimson red that extends up the sides.

HABITAT: Found in forests and cultivated fields where there is plenty of cover. Bask occasionally. Rarely if ever climb.

CAGE: Woodland with plenty of cover.

TEMPERATURE RANGE: 75-85°F.

FOOD AND WATER: Eat a variety of insects, spiders, smaller lizards, and small rodents. Supply a shallow pan of drinking water and a drip system.

SPECIAL NEEDS: Sunlight beneficial. Add vitamins and bone meal to all food.

YOUNG: Both egg-laying and live-bearing species are known. Young 4-8" at birth.

RELATED SPECIES: There are several species of galliwasps, all similar in appearance.

Chamaeleontidae

The Chameleons

The chameleons are so unique that many herpetologists feel that they deserve an order all their own alongside the lizards, snakes, and worm-lizards. The body of a chameleon is flattened laterally. Many species have a short dorsal crest, and most have some sort of a bony helmet or crest on the head. In all species there is a dewlap-like pouch that is distensible.

The eyes are mounted in fleshy turrets that have a small hole through which only the pupil is visible. The eyes are capable of independent movement. The tongue is incredibly long, often two-thirds as long as the body. When at rest, the tongue is bunched up in the throat; it is shot out at prey via muscle extension and contraction. The tip is fleshy and sticky, which helps it adhere to prey and draw it back to the mouth.

Dorsal view of the head of a chameleon showing the turreted eyes pointing in different directions. Photo by K. Lucas, Steinhart Aquarium.

The teeth are large and sharp, and the larger species can bite painfully. The tail, except in the dwarf species, is prehensile and is carried rolled up in a tight coil. It cannot be regenerated if broken. The feet are formed into pincer-like structures comprised of toes fused together in groups of two's and three's. These are used for grasping tree limbs and bushes. As chameleons are extremely slow-moving creatures, they must rely on protective coloration for defense. Most chameleons have the ability to change their color, but each species will have only a certain range of colors at its disposal. Color changes are brought on by excitement, breeding, temperature, lighting conditions, rival males, and other factors. Chameleons are extremely difficult to keep alive for any length of time in captivity. They are both egg-layers and live-bearers.

JACKSON'S CHAMELEON
(Chamaeleo jacksonii)

DISTRIBUTION: Africa.

LENGTH: 8-12".

DESCRIPTION: The Jackson's chameleon is an extraordinary animal reminiscent of the ancient dinosaur *Triceratops*. The species is sexually dimorphic, the male being the more outstanding. There are three large horns on the head of the male, one before each eye and one on the nose. There is a crest on the head in both sexes and a dorsal crest made up of separated plate-like scales extending down the back. The body is flattened laterally. The feet are typical chameleon feet, the toes being fused together into grasping tools. The tail is long, prehensile, and usually carried in a tight coil. The eyes move independently. The tongue is extremely long and is shot out at prey. Most Jackson's chameleons are a green color when at rest but may turn a variety of colors when stimulated: yellow, olive, brown, or a pattern combining all three. Occasionally some specimens may even turn a solid black.

HABITAT: Found in elevated areas, calmly perched in small trees or bushes waiting for unsuspecting prey to come by.

CAGE: A well ventilated woodland cage with a great deal of cover.

132

Detail of the head of Jackson's chameleon. Photo by G. Marcuse.

Chameleons are easily disturbed and need to feel secure and unobserved.

TEMPERATURE RANGE: 70-80°F.

FOOD AND WATER: Eats insects and needs a wide variety in order to remain healthy. Spiders are another favorite food. Supply a large pan of water and a drip system. The cage must be sprayed twice daily as these lizards will not normally drink from a dish.

SPECIAL NEEDS: Sunlight mandatory. Vitamins and bone meal should be added to all food. Chameleons are extremely delicate lizards, but if they can be kept outside where they can live fairly naturally they will live a long time. If kept indoors the life expectancy is less than two years. I do not recommend chameleons to anyone but professional herpetologists.

YOUNG: Bear live young in embryonic sacs. Young 1-1½″ at hatching. A female in the author's care gave birth to 23 young, two of which needed assistance in escaping the membranes. Often breed in captivity.

RELATED SPECIES: All chameleons are similar, but Jackson's is the only common three-horned species.

133

COMMON CHAMELEON
(Chamaeleo chamaeleon)

DISTRIBUTION: Europe and North Africa to India.

LENGTH: 8-10".

DESCRIPTION: The common or European chameleon is the only chameleon found outside of Africa and Madagascar. The head is large and bears a bony helmet, but there are no protruding horns as in the Jackson's chameleon. The body is in the typical chameleon mold, complete with grasping feet, prehensile tail, and long protrusible tongue. The eyes move independently. Chameleons are rather boisterous, and males fight violently among themselves. They are also capable of inflicting a painful bite on a human finger. The color is usually a mottled green or olive, but the color-change range includes shades of brown, black, ivory, yellow, rust, and green.

HABITAT: The European subspecies is normally found in low bushes and thick undergrowth near wooded areas. North African subspecies are ground-dwellers, living in burrows dug in sandy soil.

CAGE: Woodland, but best kept in an outdoor enclosure with living plants and bushes.

TEMPERATURE RANGE: 70-80°F.

FOOD AND WATER: Eats insects, spiders, and other small invertebrates. Supply a large pan of water and a drip system. Spray the cage daily.

SPECIAL NEEDS: Sunlight mandatory. Add vitamins and bone meal to the food given to the insects.

YOUNG: Egg-layers, prefer sandy soil for laying. Young 1-1½" at hatching. Young of all chameleons are difficult to raise unless an abundant supply of tiny insect food is available.

RELATED SPECIES: The common chameleon is the only chameleon imported from Europe. Most other chameleons are of similar shape.

Xantusiidae

The Night Lizards

The night lizards are an exclusively American family comprised of small, rather nondescript nocturnal species. They show characteristics of the geckos, teiids, and skinks. The skin is soft as in geckos and is covered with small tubercular scales. The tail is long, thick, and may be regenerated if broken. The eyes are lidless and are covered with a transparent scale; they have vertical pupils, indicating night vision.

The tongue is long, flat, and fleshy. Night lizards are said to clean the eyes with the tongue, but I have never seen this happen. All species are extremely small and secretive, venturing from their desert hiding places only at night to feed. All species are primarily terrestrial, but they may climb onto boulders or cliffs to hide in crevices or up yucca plants to hide beneath the bark. Some species burrow or hide in the burrows of larger animals. These animals are truly viviparous, the young developing inside the mother's body and attached by an umbilical cord.

DESERT NIGHT LIZARD
(Xantusia vigilis)

DISTRIBUTION: Southwestern North America.

LENGTH: 3-4".

DESCRIPTION: The desert night lizard is a tiny nocturnal reptile from the desert Southwest. The body is cylindrical and covered dorsally with tiny pebble-like scales and soft flabby skin like that of the geckos, but the scales on the belly are large and plate-like. The legs are short but powerful. The tail is long and thick and is used for fat storage; it may be broken and regenerated in an emergency. The pupil of the eye is vertical,

Xantusia vigilis, the desert night lizard. Photo by K. Lucas, Steinhart Aquarium.

indicating night vision, although these lizards may also be found abroad during the day. The eye is covered by a clear scale as in most geckos, and there are no movable eyelids. The back is gray-green with small black spots. The spots continue down the tail, which is usually yellow-green, and the belly is white.

HABITAT: Found in rock crevices, beneath rocks, or beneath the bark of yucca plants.

CAGE: Desert with several plants.

TEMPERATURE RANGE: 70-80°F.

FOOD AND WATER: Small insects, spiders, and other small invertebrates are the primary diet. Supply a small dish of drinking water and spray one or two rocks in the cage each evening.

SPECIAL NEEDS: Sunlight not necessary. Add vitamins and bone meal to the diet of the insects.

YOUNG: Live-bearers, young 3/4 to 7/8" at birth.

RELATED SPECIES: There are several species of night lizards that are all similar in appearance, but each has its own unique coloration.

136

Xenosauridae

The Xenosaurs

The xenosaurs are a rarely collected and hence a rarely seen group of unusual lizards. The body is short and stout, the legs short, powerful, and strongly clawed. The tail is moderately long and in the rare Chinese genus bears two rows of large plate-like scales. The head is covered with small scales and is triangular in shape. These lizards are live-bearers.

There are two genera of xenosaurs. One genus is Mexican and is semi-arboreal, living in bushes and tree stumps in the mountain forests of the area. The other genus is located in China and is semi-aquatic, living along the banks of mountain streams and rivers. These Chinese creatures are extremely rare in Western collections. Both genera have sharp, backward-curving teeth and bite readily.

MEXICAN XENOSAURS
(*Xenosaurus* spp.)

DISTRIBUTION: Mexico.
LENGTH: 8-10".
DESCRIPTION: Xenosaurs are rarely seen in captivity and hence are not well-known among reptile keepers. The head is triangular and fairly flat with powerful jaws and a willingness to bite. The body is flattened dorso-laterally and covered with small scales interspersed with larger beaded scales. The tail is round and of medium length. There is a row of bead-like scales down the spine forming a very short dorsal crest. The eye is bright yellow-orange or red-orange. The main body color is dark brown with lighter stripes and mottlings, and the

tail is banded with brown and yellow. These lizards are most active early in the morning and late in the evening.

HABITAT: Live in the mountain cloud forests of south-central Mexico. Prefer hollow logs or a hole beneath the roots of trees. Rarely bask in the open.

CAGE: Rain-forest with plenty of cover.

TEMPERATURE RANGE: 65-80°F.

FOOD AND WATER: Natural diet is ants, termites, and other small insects. Prefer ants in captivity or small crickets. Supply a large pan of water for drinking and bathing. A drip system is beneficial.

SPECIAL NEEDS: Sunlight probably beneficial. Add vitamins and bone meal to the food given to the crickets and ants.

YOUNG: Live-bearers, young 1½-2″ at birth.

RELATED SPECIES: There are several species of *Xenosaurus*, all of which are similar in appearance and habits.

Detail of the head of the Mexican beaded lizard, *Heloderma horridum.* Photo by K. Lucas, Steinhart Aquarium. On the facing page are shown two views of the lower jaw of *Heloderma;* with a little imagination the grooves on the teeth can just be discerned.

Helodermatidae

The Beaded Lizards

The beaded lizards are the only known poisonous lizards in the world. The poison is neurotoxic, attacking the nervous system and causing paralysis. The venom glands are located in the lower jaw and the lower teeth are grooved, which allows the poison to enter the wound. The amount of venom "injected" varies with the amount of chewing the animal does. The poison is deadly to the small animals on which the lizards feed. There is no specific antidote for the venom of these lizards.

The head is short, blunt, and flattened, the body stout and cylindrical. The legs are short, strongly muscled, and heavily clawed. The tail is moderately long and heavy and is used as a reservoir for

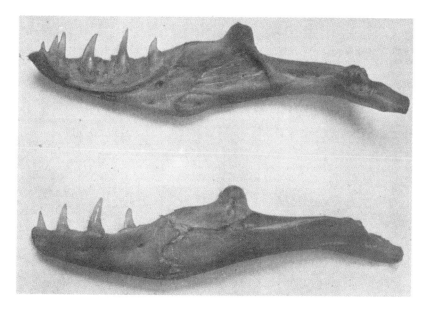

fat and water. The scales are small and tubercular, resembling beadwork. The beaded lizards are desert dwellers and can endure long periods without water. They are highly tolerant of temperature fluctuations and, although they rarely encounter standing water in their natural habitat, they love to bathe and swim. These lizards are normally slow-moving but can turn and bite rapidly, so they should never be handled.

GILA MONSTER
(Heloderma suspectum)

DISTRIBUTION: Southwestern U.S. and Mexico.

LENGTH: 18-24".

DESCRIPTION: The gila monster and the beaded lizard are the only known poisonous lizards. The head is large and flat with strong jaws, the lower ones equipped with venom-producing glands. The body is round and very stout, as is the tail. The tail is used as storage for fat and cannot be regenerated if broken. The legs are strong but fairly short, and the toes are strongly clawed. The body is covered with bead-like scales colored in a pink or salmon and black pattern. Gila monsters become fairly tame in captivity but should be handled with care and only when necessary, using the proper tools (a snake hook is ideal). Extremely hardy in captivity.

HABITAT: Found in dry arid areas with sparse vegetation. Shelter beneath rocks or in burrows. Bask occasionally and are often active at night.

CAGE: Desert.

TEMPERATURE RANGE: 75-85°F.

FOOD AND WATER: Eat insects, spiders, small lizards, birds, rodents, and eggs. Supply a large pan of water as these lizards love to soak and swim. Drip system may be beneficial.

SPECIAL NEEDS: Sunlight beneficial. Add plenty of vitamins and bone meal to all foods.

YOUNG: Egg-layers, prefer holes in sandy soil for laying. Young 6-8" at hatching.

RELATED SPECIES: Beaded lizard.

MEXICAN BEADED LIZARD
(Heloderma horridum)

DISTRIBUTION: Mexico.

LENGTH: 24-30".

DESCRIPTION: The beaded lizards are large, poisonous lizards active mostly at night. The head is broad and flattened with poison glands located in the lower jaw. The body is long and heavy but not quite as stout as that of the gila monster. The legs are longer and the feet have longer claws; the tail is longer as well. In fact, the lizard looks like a gila monster that has been stretched out. The scales are bead-like and form a pattern of yellow and black stripes and mottlings; one subspecies is completely black. Beaded lizards are more irritable than gila monsters and more likely to bite. They should never be handled.

HABITAT: Found in dry arid areas with abundant rocks and sparse vegetation. Retire to burrows to avoid the midday heat.

CAGE: Desert.

TEMPERATURE RANGE: 80-90°F.

FOOD AND WATER: Eats insects, spiders, other small invertebrates, lizards, snakes, rodents, birds, and eggs. Supply a large pan of water for drinking and bathing.

SPECIAL NEEDS: Sunlight probably beneficial. Add vitamins and bone meal to all food.

YOUNG: Egg-layers, prefer burrows in sandy soil for laying. Young 6-8" at hatching.

RELATED SPECIES: Gila monster.

Remaining Families

The following groups of lizards will likely never be kept by an amateur, and even professional herpetologists may never see them. The one exception might be the shovel-snouted legless lizard, which is common in some parts of California (although facing habitat destruction in some areas). The Bornean earless monitor is not so rare as was once suspected, but its habitat is hostile and it is difficult to locate specimens when looking for them. As a result they are rare in collections. This lizard may well be a link between the lizards and snakes.

The flap-footed lizards are a unique group related to the geckos. They are confined to Australia and New Guinea. All are snake-like in appearance and bear two small remnants of hind legs, merely flaps of skin just in front of the anal opening that look like fins. All are strictly terrestrial in their habits and the majority are burrowers as well. All species lay eggs. They have lidless eyes as do the majority of the geckos; the eyes are covered with a transparent scale that is cleaned with the long flat tongue. There are both diurnal and nocturnal forms in this family. All have long tails, in some twice as long as the body; the tail may be regenerated if broken. The shovel-snouted legless lizards are a unique group of American lizards found on the West Coast. They are diminutive burrowers with no visible remnants of legs. All known species are live-bearers. The eyes are functional and have movable eyelids, there is no external ear, and the tongue is long and forked. All species burrow in loose sandy soil on beaches.

The dibamids are another group of small legless burrowers from southeastern Asia. Although quite common in their native habitat, they are rarely collected and even more rarely imported. All species are forest dwellers and lay eggs. The eyes are covered with skin as are the ears. The males have short spurs for hind legs that are probably used for gripping the female during copulation. These lizards show anatomical similarities to the geckos.

The anelytropsids are represented by one species found only a few times in Mexican deserts. It is limbless, a burrower, and may be related to the dibamids.

The feylinids are the final group of limbless burrowing lizards. These reptiles are found in African forests. There are no external ears and the eyes are covered with transparent scales. They are live-bearers.

A. LANTHANOTIDAE
BORNEAN EARLESS MONITOR
(Lanthanotus borneensis)

DISTRIBUTION: Borneo.

LENGTH: 12-18".

DESCRIPTION: These lizards are among the rarest herps in collections. They are burrowers that avoid direct sunlight and also enjoy the water, being able to remain submerged for a long period of time. The body is elongated with alternating rows of large horny scales and smaller keeled scales along the back. The legs are short but powerful. The head is similar in shape to that of the beaded lizards, but there are several differences: first, there are no external ear openings; next, the nostrils are located high on the head; and last, the lower eyelids have a transparent scale through which the lizard can see with the eyes closed. The tail is as long as the body and is incapable of regeneration if broken. The teeth are curved backward and resemble fangs. The tongue is long and forked. The color is dark gray-brown with no other markings.

HABITAT: Frequent areas surrounding the rice paddies in Borneo. Sometimes caught in nets in the paddies themselves.

CAGE: Usually kept in a terrarium with several inches of moist soil and supplied with a tank of water for swimming. Evidently these lizards are among the laziest of all animals, barely moving at all in captivity.

TEMPERATURE RANGE: 70-80°F.

FOOD AND WATER: Diet in the wild is unknown. Has been induced to eat fish, eggs, and earthworms in captivity.

YOUNG: Breeding habits unknown.

RELATED SPECIES: None.

143

B. PYGOPODIDAE
BURTON'S SCALY-FOOT
(Lialis burtonis)

DISTRIBUTION: Australia and New Guinea.

LENGTH: 18-24".

DESCRIPTION: The Burton's scaly-foot is fairly common and typical of the pygopodids, and it is also the largest and most widespread species of the family. The body is long and snake-like and, as opposed to most legless lizards, is very supple and lithe. The scales are small and fairly uniform. The head is long and pointed and the eyes are lidless, being covered by a transparent scale. The tongue is long and flat and, as in the geckos, is used to clean the eyes. The eyes have vertical pupils that would seem to indicate night vision, but these lizards may be found out foraging for food during the daylight hours as well as at night. The color pattern varies with habitat and even among individuals in the same area, but the basic color is tan or gray-brown, the lips are white, and there is a dark stripe through the eye. There are no front limbs, and the hind limbs are represented by fin-like flaps of skin.

HABITAT: Found in a wide range of habitats from desert to grass-land to the outskirts of rain-forests. Fairly secretive, hide in burrows, beneath rocks, or under bushes.

CAGE: Woodland or similar to that described for the collared lizard.

TEMPERATURE RANGE: 75-90°F.

FOOD AND WATER: Some specimens will eat insects, but the preferred diet is smaller lizards. Supply a pan of water for drinking and bathing. These lizards are difficult to keep alive and I do not recommend them as captives.

SPECIAL NEEDS: Vitamins and bone meal should be added to food. Some sunlight beneficial.

YOUNG: Egg-layers, prefer to lay in sandy soil. Young 5-6" at hatching.

RELATED SPECIES: There are several genera of scaly-foot lizards, all similar in appearance.

C. ANNIELLIDAE
SHOVEL-SNOUTED LEGLESS LIZARD
(Anniella pulchra)

DISTRIBUTION: California to Baja California.

LENGTH: 8-10".

DESCRIPTION: These lizards are legless burrowers found along the California coast. The body is long, thin, and worm-like. There are no external ears, but there are movable eyelids and functional eyes. The head is conical in shape for ease in burrowing, and the snout (as the common name indicates) is shaped like a shovel that also aids in digging. The color varies with subspecies: *Anniella pulchra pulchra* is silver-gray with dark stripes running the length of the back, the belly white or yellow; *Anniella pulchra niger* is solid black or dark brown.

HABITAT: Prefers loose, moist, sandy soil. Locally common in sand dunes bordering the beaches on the California coast. Usually found several inches underground, but will sometimes forage for food above ground when there is plenty of plant growth. Rarely if ever bask.

Detail of the head of *Anniella pulchra*. Photo by K. Lucas, Steinhart Aquarium.

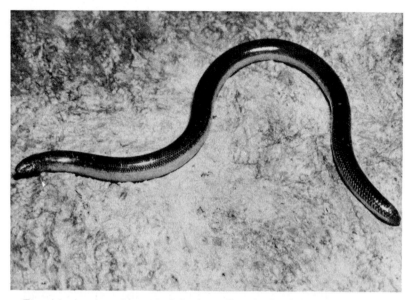

The black shovel-snouted legless lizard, *Anniella pulchra niger.*
Photo by K. Lucas, Steinhart Aquarium.

CAGE: Desert with several inches of semi-moist sand as flooring material.

TEMPERATURE RANGE: 70-80°F.

FOOD AND WATER: Eats small insects in the wild and in captivity. Supply a small shallow dish of drinking water.

SPECIAL NEEDS: Sunlight not mandatory. Vitamins and calcium-rich food should be fed to all insects.

YOUNG: Live-bearers, young 2-2½" at birth.

RELATED SPECIES: Another species occurs in Baja California.

D. DIBAMIDAE

DISTRIBUTION: Southeastern Asia through Indonesia and New Guinea.

LENGTH: 6-12".

DESCRIPTION: These small burrowing lizards are not particularly rare but are rarely seen due to their secretive habits in Asian rain-forests. The shape is like that of a large worm;

there are no front limbs, but males have tiny spurs for hind legs. The eyes are small and covered with skin, and there are no external ears. The color is brown or purplish brown. They do well in a cage full of moist earth covered with bark, kept at a temperature of 75-80 °F., and supplied with a dish of water. They eat worms and small insects encountered while burrowing. Egg-layers, lay in tunnels underground. Possibly related to the anelytropsids.

E. ANELYTROPSIDAE

DISTRIBUTION: Mexico.
LENGTH: 6-8".
DESCRIPTION: The anelytropsids are known only from a handful of specimens found in the deserts of Mexico. They are blind, legless burrowers, yellow-brown in color. If more specimens are found we may discover how to keep them in captivity. Probably eat termites and ants in the wild. Breeding habits unknown.

F. FEYLINIDAE

DISTRIBUTION: Africa.
LENGTH: 12-14".
DESCRIPTION: The feylinids are burrowing lizards from tropical Africa. The head is flattened and the body is wormlike, both adaptations for a subterranean existence. There are no external ears, and the eyes are hidden beneath transparent scales. There are no external traces of legs. The color is solid brown. They eat termites almost exclusively and can be kept as the dibamids. These lizards are live-bearers and are possibly related to the skinks.

Left: A cage for large semi-aquatic lizards. **Below:** A rain-forest cage. Photos by the author.

Housing

In the area of housing the best rule of thumb is the larger the cage the better. There are basically two types of lizard cages into which can be incorporated one of the three main habitats in which lizards are found in the wild.

THE GLASS TANK

The traditional "cage" for reptiles is an aquarium. I recommend these only for indoor use and then only when inclement weather prevents keeping the lizards outdoors.

Most aquariums are simply five panes of glass glued together inside a frame of stainless steel or plastic. As long as there are no sharp exposed edges, either frame is satisfactory. A screen top may be used to keep your captives captive.

THE WOODEN CAGE

The wooden frame cage covered in screen wire is the ideal home for nearly all lizards. Most lizards (but not all) will learn not to rub their noses on the screen. Nervous varieties are best kept in glass tanks. The wooden cage allows the circulation of fresh air and admission of sunlight, including essential ultraviolet rays. Also, these cages cost much less than glass tanks and may be built to your exact specifications.

HABITATS
(1) THE DESERT CAGE

The desert cage is suitable for all those lizards that have a dry heat requirement of 85° and over. The ideal flooring medium is ordinary fine-grained sand. Rocks and wood may be added for hiding and basking places. I do not recommend the use of cactus plants for two reasons. One, the lizards will dig up and destroy the cactus, and two, the lizards will pick up spines that are difficult to remove.

A typical desert cage with numerous boulders for use as basking sites. Photo by the author.

The desert tank will need artificial heat even when placed outdoors except during the warm summer months in the South. I recommend the use of ordinary incandescent light bulbs or infrared lamps that may be placed on the cage to help you regulate the temperature. Keep it about 90-95°F. Recently a substratum heating cord has been introduced that is very effective for heating the flooring material, but it does not have the ability to heat the air in the cage.

The desert tank must be kept absolutely dry. Most desert lizards will become sluggish, refuse to eat, and finally die in a damp cage.

Use a small dish for those lizards that will drink standing water, but keep the edge of the container about ½" above the surface of the sand in order to minimize the amount of sand in the water and water on the sand. The water should be changed daily.

(2) THE WOODLAND CAGE

The woodland cage is suitable for those lizards that require dry warmth yet enjoy the opportunity to climb. The flooring medium should be blasting sand or ordinary potting soil at a depth of 2-3", which will facilitate the burrowing tendencies of some species. Rocks, artificial plants, and tree limbs may be added to afford the animals a choice of basking and resting places.

A large container of water with a depth of 2" should be placed in the cage. Several rocks (granite or flint is ideal, as sedimentary rocks often pollute the water and make it unpalatable) should be placed in the water so smaller lizards will not drown if they fall in.

The woodland cage and the following type may be combined into one if the cage is fairly large.

(3) RAIN-FOREST CAGE

The rain-forest cage is suitable for those lizards that require either more humidity, actual moisture, or more shade than the desert or woodland cage can provide.

The ideal flooring material is peat moss or potting soil. An abundance of rocks, logs, branches, and artificial plants should be placed in the cage to provide hiding places and shelter from too-intense heat and light. A "drip system" should be maintained in this type of cage. This is simply an arrangement by which a steady drip of water splashes into the water container for several hours each day. The benefit of this system is two-fold. First, if the drip is directed onto a plant or branch and allowed to run off into the water container, lizards that will not drink standing water will lap up the single drops. Second, the fine mist from the splashing will create a moister, more humid environment.

SPECIALTY CAGES

Certain lizards, especially some of the larger varieties, require special cages. These are all covered in the individual description sections.

CAGE ACCESSORIES
(1) FLOORING MEDIUM

The key word here is clean. Sand and blasting sand (aquarium

151

gravel) should be washed thoroughly before use. Prepackaged potting soil and peat moss are usually sterile and safe to use right from the package. Regardless of the medium used, the depth should average 2-3″ and should be kept fairly free of debris and excrement. I recommend cleaning the material every two weeks and total replacement every three months.

(2) ROCKS

Any type of rock is fine for the dry area of your cage. Flat rocks are ideal and allow for stacking into miniature cliffs. These are ideal for all secretive lizards. Be absolutely certain that the rocks are steady and cannot collapse on your captives. I once lost a beautiful chuckwalla by neglecting this.

(3) WOOD

Any type of wooden accessory such as bark, logs, branches, etc. can be used in your cage. However, be sure that there are no unnatural sharp edges that may injure your captives. Also, it is wise to clean the material thoroughly if it may have been exposed to any spray or pesticides.

(4) PLANTS

As I have mentioned previously, I do not recommend the use of live plants in lizard cages. There are several reasons for this, regarding the welfare of both the lizards and the plants. First, most lizards will dig up the living plants and kill them. Second, some lizards eat plants, and nearly all houseplants will have pesticide residues on them which are detrimental to reptiles. Third, most houseplants will wither and die in the enclosed environment of a lizard cage. Fourth, spiny plants such as thorn bushes or cacti may injure your specimens.

I recommend the use of plastic plants for four reasons. First, the plastic plants are non-toxic as long as they are washed thoroughly before use. Second, they are easy to keep clean and require no other care. Third, they may be fastened down to prevent unauthorized relandscaping. Fourth, they always present a lush, attractive appearance and serve as excellent shelters and basking places. Also, lizards make no distinction between real and plastic plants and more than likely do not know that the plants are artificial.

A drip bottle system using an I.V. bag and a manually regulated valve. Photo by the author.

(5) WATER DISH AND DRIP SYSTEM

Almost any container will do for a water dish as long as it is fairly large, shallow, heavy enough to avoid tipping, and made of a non-toxic material. Glass, crockery, wooden bowls, plastic bowls, or aluminum baking pans are all satisfactory. A two-inch water depth is ideal, and non-sedimentary rocks should be placed in the water dish.

The water itself may be ordinary tap water if allowed to stand for 24 hours. I encourage all lizard keepers to put a cuttlebone in the dish in order to get enough calcium into your animals' diets.

The drip system should be a fairly simple arrangement. The best situation is one in which an ordinary garden hose is allowed to drip slowly into a water basin equipped with a drain. This may be left to run 24 hours a day so there is no reason to ever change

153

the water. However, as utility bills continue to climb, an infinitely more pactical setup is to obtain a standard hospital I.V. bag fitted with a manually regulated valve; fill the bag with clean water and set the valve to allow for one drop every two seconds. This should last between four and five hours with a standard size bag. The drip should be directed onto a branch or plant and allowed to fall into the water pan from the obstacle.

(6) ARTIFICIAL LIGHT

Lizards kept indoors during the winter need artificial lighting to simulate natural sunlight, as they need the ultraviolet light the sun provides in order to produce essential vitamin D3 in their bodies. For ordinary heat and light use incandescent light bulbs. For ultraviolet light use one of the special bulbs designed for use with houseplants and home aquariums. "Blacklight" bulbs do not supply the entire spectrum of ultraviolet light needed for D3 production and are therefore ineffective.

THE COMMUNITY CAGE

Many species of lizards, especially the smaller varieties, may be kept together in one cage. There are several rules to follow in this situation. First, never overcrowd your captives. Eight inches of lizard to two square feet of cage space is a good rule, though more is preferable if possible, especially for strictly terrestrial species. Second, only put lizards that require the same type of environment together. Third, only put lizards that are of like size together or you may discover only one very fat happy lizard in the cage.

Food And Nutrition

(1) CRICKETS

Crickets are an ideal food for nearly all lizard species, even those that are normally vegetarians. These insects are soft-bodied and provide most essential nutrients. Further, crickets are fairly easy to raise if preparations are made well in advance of your lizard acquisitions and if you have the space.

To raise crickets I recommend obtaining a large aquarium fitted with a fine mesh top. Place several inches of ordinary topsoil in the tank and place several large pieces of bark on the earth to provide nesting places. Next place several layers of old egg cartons on one side of the tank to provide hiding spots. A dish should be sunk flush with the soil and filled with fine chicken mash into which a pet vitamin tonic and powdered bone meal have been mixed. This will provide the crickets, and in turn the lizards, with a nutritious diet. Water should be supplied via a commercial chicken waterer.

Many lizards will eat only other lizards. Usually the most common local lizard is the cheapest to obtain in quantity. Shown is *Urosaurus ornatus,* a common western American lizard often used as food. Photo by K. Lucas, Steinhart Aquarium.

If this colony is not heavily depleted, crickets of various sizes and stages of development should soon be prevalent in the tank. Such a colony should maintain itself indefinitely. If crickets are to be purchased periodically rather than raised, the same style tank may be used.

(2) MEALWORMS

These are the larvae of a common beetle. They possess hard, chitinous exoskeletons that may clog the intestines of your lizards if fed to them as an exclusive diet. However, mealworms are rich in amino acids and proteins and are good for an occasional variation in diet. They, like crickets, are readily accepted by almost all lizards.

(3) OTHER INSECTS

I tend to avoid wild-caught insects as lizard food because of the possibility of pesticide poisoning. However, if the insects are captured fairly far away from residential districts and farms, they are excellent for diet variation. Grasshoppers are especially good, as are fruit flies.

(4) EARTHWORMS

Comparatively few lizards will accept earthworms. Notable exceptions are several species of Asian agamids. Each commercial worm dealer will have his own suggestions for proper care and breeding of earthworms.

(5) REPTILES

Many lizards feed almost exclusively on other lizards and small snakes. Good "food lizards" are small fence swifts (*Sceloporus* spp.), green anoles *(Anolis carolinensis)*, side-blotched lizards *(Uta stansburniana)*, and sand lizards (*Holbrookia* spp.). Good "food snakes" are ringnecks, ground snakes, and small garter snakes.

(6) MICE AND RATS

These rodents are excellent food for larger lizards. They may be purchased frozen in quantity from biological supply houses. I recommend you feed only dead rodents to lizards as live ones will often turn the tables and may make a meal of your captives.

Rodents are an excellent nutritional source for lizards, especially when they themselves have been fed a high-protein high-calcium diet. Pet dealers will be more than happy to give you tips on raising these rodents.

156

Grasshoppers are found everywhere and are taken by many types of lizards. Photo by Muller-Schmida.

(7) BEEF AND PORK

I do not recommend the use of these foods for captive lizards as the fat content is usually too high.

(8) EGGS

Several species of larger lizards are fond of eggs, but I recommend them only in moderation as excessive amounts of egg whites can disrupt a lizard's digestive tract.

(9) PLANT FOOD

Vegetarian lizards normally eat a wide variety of plant foods in the wild and will thrive best in captivity under the same conditions. Leafy green vegetables are readily accepted but offer little nutrition. Fruits, vegetables, flowers, and greens of certain wildflowers such as dandelions offer more nutrition and are readily accepted. Any wild plants or store-bought vegetables and fruit should be washed thoroughly to remove any pesticide residue. A pet vitamin tonic and powdered bone meal should be added to the plant material before feeding.

(10) SPECIALTY FOODS

These are mentioned in the individual description sections where applicable.

(11) DIETARY SUPPLEMENTS

I recommend that all captive reptiles be given plenty of powdered bone meal to provide enough calcium for strong bone tissue. Also, I suggest that a vitamin tonic rich in vitamin D3 be added to your captives' diets.

FORCE-FEEDING

Almost all lizards will eat readily when supplied with their natural diet. However, occasional individuals refuse to eat when first captured and may require force-feeding before adapting to captivity and feeding on their own.

I do not recommend or condone force-feeding as a continued practice. It is best to turn such animals loose in their native habitat or donate them to an institution rather than continually disturbing and frightening them. Exceptions would be only very rare or very expensive specimens.

To force-feed, grasp the lizard gently but firmly behind the jaws and apply slight pressure until the jaws open. Then push the food well back into the lizard's mouth and allow the jaws to close over the item. If pushed far enough back into the mouth, the food will usually be swallowed. This method is also effective for administering oral medication or vitamin supplements. Make certain any insects or other animals used in force-feeding are dead before feeding because the lizard probably will swallow without first chewing and crushing. A live insect or lizard in the stomach of your captive can cause a great deal of internal damage before expiring.

Care of Young and Eggs

Occasionally, under the best of conditions, captive lizards will breed and produce fertile eggs or live young. Additionally, some lizards may already be pregnant when caught or purchased. This may be fortunate indeed if you are prepared for it, especially with the rarer and lesser known species. This may be very unfortunate if you are not prepared for it.

This section is designed to instruct the reader how to breed lizards, how to prepare for the arrival of the eggs or young, how to hatch the eggs, and how to feed and care for the young.

BREEDING LIZARDS

First of all, lizards will not breed unless they want to. The trick here is making them want to, short of using perfume and eye shadow.

Copulation in *Lacerta* is typical of mating in all lizards. Photo by W. Lierath.

Determine that you have a male and female or females. Many lizards show sexual dimorphism in the brighter colors, longer claws, higher dorsal crests, larger dewlaps, and swollen tail bases of the males. One sure way of determining sex is by gently squeezing on both sides of the tail base. If the animal is a male, the hemipenes may be seen inside the cloaca or may actually protrude. The female will have no such organs.

After sexing the animals, prepare a cage for them to use exclusively which simulates their natural habitat as closely as possible. Provide plenty of vitamins and calcium-rich food and wait for results. Avoid disturbing the lizards if at all possible, and their attention will be directed toward each other rather than you.

Each species of lizard will have its own special courtship ritual, but the end result is copulation, which is fairly universal in procedure. The male grasps the female's neck in his mouth, swings his tail under hers until cloacas meet, and inserts one hemipene into the female. The pair may remain in this posture for only a few seconds or several minutes, depending upon the species. This process may be repeated as often as the female remains receptive.

Once fertilized, the female will increase in girth rapidly and eat more often. Highly nutritious, calcium-rich food should be given to the female throughout her pregnancy along with as much sunlight as possible to ensure the probability of strong hard-shelled eggs and healthy infants.

PREPARATION OF NESTING SITE
AND CARE OF EGGS

Many egg-laying lizards require specific nesting areas or materials. Unless these are provided the female may refuse to lay and will ultimately die egg-bound. Other varieties will lay anywhere regardless of what materials are supplied. Unfortunately, this often leads to the lizards laying in their water bowls, so during the last stages of pregnancy supply the female with drinking water only twice a day, in the morning and evening; make certain she drinks deeply both times. Supply the female with an area of moist (but not wet) soft earth and sphagnum moss sheltered by branches and plants. A hollow log filled with moss and earth is ideal. If laid outside during the summer, kept from direct sunlight, and not allowed to dry out, the eggs will hatch naturally.

160

Egg clutch of *Lacerta*. Lizard eggs are often round and usually white.
Photo by W. Lierath.

During the winter the eggs may be hatched artificially. Place several inches of moist earth and sphagnum moss into a gallon jar and place the eggs in the jar on top of the soil, not beneath it. Place a lid on the jar with a few air holes to allow for circulation. Cover the jar with paper or cloth and maintain it at a temperature of 75-80 °F. Check the eggs periodically for signs of mold or mildew, clean them of debris if necessary, and change the flooring material. Also, do not allow the soil to become too dry. Lizard eggs lose moisture quickly, and once they wrinkle it is doubtful if they can be revived. Lizards, excluding geckos, lay leathery soft-shelled eggs that are easily damaged, so handle with care. Gecko eggs are hard-shelled and not as easily harmed.

LIVE-BEARING LIZARDS

These lizards will drop their youngsters anywhere and rarely will the female pay any attention to them. However, after a few days of annoyance she may eat them and the male certainly will, so

161

Varanus storri, a small (under one foot) monitor from northern Australia (Varanidae). Photo by H. Frauca.

Varanus salvator, the water monitor (Varanidae). Photo by H. Hansen, Aquarium Berlin.

Tiliqua scincioides, a blue-tongue skink (Scincidae). Photo by Dr. S. A. Minton.

Eumeces fasciatus, the five-lined skink (Scincidae). Photo by K. Lucas, Steinhart Aquarium. The double tail is the result of an incomplete breakage followed by regeneration, thus the original tail is present and so is a smaller regenerated one.

Eggs and hatchlings of *Sceloporus magister,* a fence swift. Photo by K. Lucas, Steinhart Aquarium.

it is best to remove the infants immediately after birth. Most live-bearers eject the young fully developed and also eject the embryonic sacs as well. Other live-bearers give birth to young still contained within individual egg sacs. These normally are opened within a few seconds by the infants; however, some specimens require a little help. Once the sac is split open, it may be gently and slowly pulled away from the infant.

CARE OF NEWBORN YOUNG

After isolating the young from their parents, offer them drops of water on a leaf or rock. Provide them with small insects such as baby crickets or fruit flies. Infant lizards are able to forage for themselves at birth and require no special maternal attention as do baby mammals and birds.

The main problem with raising these infants is supplying them with enough food of small size and high nutrition. It is best to plan the food supply well in advance of hatching in order to build up a colony of flies or newborn crickets, since acquiring these during the winter months is difficult if not completely impossible. Lizards grow quickly during their first few months, and the sooner they will accept adult foods the better.

Diseases

The lizards are subject to a variety of diseases both in the wild and in captivity. Rarely, however, will a sick lizard be encountered in the wild, for nature rarely tolerates a weakened animal for long.

In captivity the situation is somewhat different. In a cage a lizard faces no natural predators and if sick and untreated will die a slow and painful death. To combat this possibility, you will find here listed a number of common minor disorders and the best methods of treating them before they become major problems. All sick lizards should be isolated from their cagemates.

(1) MALNUTRITION

Many store-bought lizards may appear rather skinny and listless when first purchased. If not too far gone, they may be brought back to health by first supplying them with a warm, dry cage with a large dish full of cool, clean water. Next, dust an abundance of food with bone meal and vitamins and feed the lizards as often as they will eat until they begin to fill out—overfeed them. When weight begins to show in the tail, the thighs, and the neck you may put the animals on a normal dietary schedule and introduce them into their permanent home.

(2) MOUTH ROT

This is a very common ailment in captive lizards. It is especially prevalent in iguanids, agamids, and teiids. The initial infection is evidently started by a strain of bacteria. This will result in a small crusty spot on or in the lizard's mouth. If discoverd at this stage and treated immediately, a quick recovery is assured. However, if undetected the lesion will become puffy and white with a fungus-like appearance. This will spread quickly and ultimately kill the animal, not by itself, but the animal will refuse to eat and drink because of the pain.

If caught in the early stages, the infection may be cured by an application of common 2% Mercurochrome. If this does not work (it usually does) use a stronger antibiotic product such as Pelizone

Egernia cunninghamii, the spiny-tailed skink (Scincidae). Photo by Dr. O. Klee.

Mabuya striata, a rainbow skink (Scincidae). Photo by H. Hansen, Aquarium Berlin.

Egernia whitii, White's skink (Scincidae). Photo by Dr. S. A. Minton. This southeastern Australian species requires a less stringently dry habitat than the related but very different spiny-tailed skink.

Cordylus warrenii depressus, the spotted girdle-tail (Cordylidae). Photo by A. Norman.

ointment or Sulfe-Met, both of which are available from a veterinarian.

(3) EYE INFECTIONS

Although more common in turtles, these infections sometimes occur in lizards. Normally they may be cleared up by gently swabbing the eye with warm water and applying a fungicide remedy specifically designed for this purpose, such as Gantrisin or Terramycin.

(4) CUTS AND ABRASIONS

Minor cuts and scrapes may be treated as you would treat your own. Wash the wound with warm water and mild soap. Then apply a topical antibiotic such as Mercurochrome. If the wound is liable to collect dirt, isolate the animal in a clean cage with newspaper as flooring material until a full scab appears over the wound. The lizard may then be returned to its usual cage.

For larger cuts or really serious wounds, broken bones, or bites, treat the wound with soap and water and then contact a veterinarian for further assistance. Normally your nearest zoo or natural history museum will be able to furnish you with the name of a good doctor who handles reptiles.

(5) INTERNAL PARASITES

These are extremely difficult to treat. Common roundworms may be eliminated by using commercial "wormers" for dogs and cats in diluted dosages. If it becomes apparent that the animal is suffering badly from internal causes consult a veterinarian. If he is unable to cure the animal it is best to destroy it as humanely as possible. The best way is to place the lizard in a plastic bag and freeze it. It is doubtful that the animal actually suffers this way.

(6) EXTERNAL PARASITES

Ticks, mites, and, in some semi-aquatic species, leeches are the only external parasites that normally attack lizards. Ticks are usually easy to see and may be removed from the lizard with tweezers or forceps using a slow steady pull. The head will normally come with the body unless jerked. After removal, swab the area with alcohol and forget about it.

Leeches may be removed in the same manner as ticks. Both parasites are best killed while still in the forceps by burning them with a match or cigarette lighter.

168

Regeneration of tails seldom presents problems with infection in most lizards. The regenerated tail is of course almost never as nice as the original.

Mites are small parasites that look much like small red spiders, to which they and ticks are related. Mites annoy reptiles much as fleas annoy mammals and are just as difficult to eliminate.

Most pesticides are just as harmful to reptiles as they are to the parasites, so I do not recommend their use. Probably the best way to kill mites is to fully submerge the infested lizard in a container of warm water for a few seconds. This will dislodge and drown the mites. Also, the cage in which the animal was kept should be thoroughly cleaned and the flooring material replaced.

(7) RUBBER JAW

Specimens that have not received enough sunlight (specifically ultraviolet light) and calcium will develop a weakening of the bone tissues, and the bones of the jaws and feet may feel somewhat flexible if the malady has set in. In extreme cases the lizard may develop rickets. Both can be cured by plenty of exposure to sunlight and a high-calcium and high-protein diet. Although the decalcification will reverse itself and the bones will reharden, any deformities that may have developed will remain.

Cordylus giganteus, the sungazer (Cordylidae). Photo by H. Hansen, Aquarium Berlin.

Platysaurus sp., a flat lizard (Cordylidae). Photo by G. S. Axelrod.

Phelsuma madagascariensis, the Madagascar day gecko (Gekkonidae).

Gekko gecko, tokay geckos (Gekkonidae). Photo by H. Hansen, Aquarium Berlin.

Lizards are found in almost all temperate to tropical habitats, but the life history and behavior of even the most common are seldom fully understood. There is much chance for careful amateurs to make noteworthy observations in these and related fields. Photo by Dr. O. Klee of *Varanus niloticus* habitat in western Africa.

Field Work

One of the best ways to learn about lizards is to observe them and/or collect them in the wild. Since most amateurs will not have the opportunity to study exotic lizards in their natural habitats, I will mention only the best methods for collecting and observing native species.

AREAS AND TECHNIQUES
FOR OBSERVATION AND COLLECTION

Almost any natural unspoiled area may have its complement of lizards. The arid, rocky climes of our southwestern states are excellent study areas for native desert species. During the day chuckwallas, desert iguanas, collared and leopard lizards, horned lizards, and other small iguanids may be seen scampering over rocks or basking in the sun. Whiptails may be seen streaking from bush to bush in search of insect prey. In the early morning and late afternoon, desert skinks may make their appearance, keeping close to rock crevices and other hiding places. At night, banded geckos and night lizards emerge and forage for food, often seeking out large flat rocks and, sometimes unfortunately, roads for warmth.

Woodlands also offer a diversity of species for observation. In the deep woods small skinks abound beneath rocks, logs, and leaf litter. Prime target areas, however, are the edges of woods where fence swifts, whiptails, glass lizards, and skinks hunt for food and frequently bask in the open.

The most effective and simplest technique for observation of lizards is also the best for collection. Binoculars are helpful in spotting the animals some distance away in order to plan your approach. When a lizard is spotted, approach it from an angle and never look directly at it. Most animals have a "flight zone" which is simply that area around the animal which when entered into

173

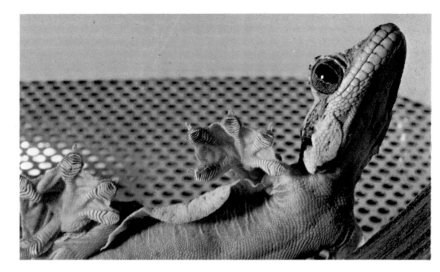

Ptychozoon kuhlii, a flying gecko (Gekkonidae). Photo by K. Lucas, Steinhart Aquarium.

Hemidactylus persicus, the Persian gecko, a close relative of the Turkish gecko (Gekkonidae). Photo by Dr. S. A. Minton.

Gerrhonotus kingi, an alligator lizard (Anguinidae). Photo by F. J. Dodd, Jr.

Ophisaurus apodus, the sheltopusik (Anguinidae). Photo by J. K. Langhammer.

will cause the animal to flee. Most smaller lizards may be approached to within four to six feet; larger species have an expanded zone. For simpler observation, keep at least five feet out of this area, settle quietly, and do not make any sudden moves. The lizards will probably continue their normal activities and pay no attention to you.

For collection, follow the procedure described above and slowly move into the flight zone, watching the lizard out of the corner of your eye. Then either make a quick grab for the animal with your hand (avoiding the tail) or use one of the collecting tools described in the next section.

For collecting the more secretive diurnal lizards overturn rocks, logs, trash, and other debris on the ground. Loose bark near the base of large trees may also shelter lizards. Most exposed lizards freeze momentarily and may be quickly grabbed. One must be careful not to grab too quickly, however, because copperheads, coral snakes, and other poisonous animals may also be under the object you overturn.

For collecting nocturnal species, a flashlight or head lantern is the only real tool needed. Road hunting is especially effective for geckos, as their eyes will reflect a red-orange luminescence from your flashlight. The light tends to momentarily blind the lizards, and they normally can be picked up by hand.

TOOLS AND CONTAINERS FOR COLLECTING

The best tools for collecting most lizards are your bare hands. However, for those lizards that are more wary and fleet of foot a collecting noose or net may be necessary. I personally use a noose, as a net may frighten the lizard or if netted the animal may simply run up the side of the net and make a flying leap to freedom.

The collecting noose is a simple affair consisting of an old fishing rod and heavy monofilament line, preferably 20-lb. test. I resist using wire as it may cut into the flesh of the animals. Attach one end of the line to the tip of the rod and fashion a slip knot that will act as the noose. Run the other end of the line down the pole, through the eyelets, and leave it unattached. Most basking lizards will ignore the transparent noose being placed over their heads and will sit quietly until you pull the loop tight with the free end of the line. You have just captured a lizard.

176

A good strong flashlight is indispensable for night hunting, as are binoculars for day hunting.

Captives may be placed in several types of containers for transportation in the field. The best is an old flour sack or pillow case that may be knotted at the top and thrust up under your belt, leaving your hands free to catch something else. Smaller specimens may be placed in plastic water jugs or cardboard shoe boxes that have been ventilated. Under no circumstances should any collecting bag or box be left in the sun unattended or in a closed parked car, unless, of course, you enjoy fried lizard.

Regardless of which type collecting container you use, transport your captives to their new homes as quickly as possible to avoid shock and exhaustion from frantic escape attempts. Also, never over-collect. Just capture those specimens that you can comfortably maintain.

A Closing Word

There are two good reasons for keeping lizards in captivity. One is for pleasure, the enjoyment of the animal itself and its uniqueness. The second reason is to study the animals and learn more about them and their habits.

One of the best ways to learn more about lizards in captivity is to observe them closely over a long period of time. Study feeding habits, threat diplays, courting and territorial disputes. Keep notes on food consumed, growth, color changes, and gestation periods. Note number of eggs and young and size of each. Keep records on virtually anything you feel could add to our knowledge of these fascinating reptiles. Some of the most informative and important scientific discoveries and subsequent papers have come from such observations.

Mating and birth in the slowworm, *Anguis fragilis* (Anguinidae): 1) Mating; 2) detail of male's hold on female's head; 3) newly born young. Photos by D. Poisson, courtesy Nancy Aquarium, France.

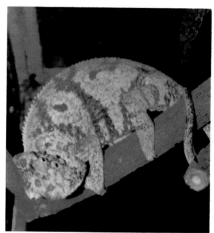

Right: *Chamaeleo chamaeleon,* the common chameleon (Chamaeleontidae). Photo by H. Hansen, Aquarium Berlin. **Below:** Jackson's chameleon, *Chamaeleo jacksonii* (Chamaeleontidae). Photo by J. Bridges.

Glossary

Anterior: Pertaining to the front end.

Aquatic: Living primarily in the water.

Arboreal: Living primarily in the trees.

Carnivorous: Feeding strictly on other animals and/or their eggs.

Caudal: Pertaining to the tail.

Cloaca: The organ, roughly analogous to the rectum in mammals, into which the urinary, digestive, and reproductive organs deposit their products. This opens to the outside via the anal opening.

Convergent evolution: Unrelated species developing like appearance and/or habits in widely separated areas.

Crest: A row of separate, extended, regular scales on the middorsal surface of a lizard.

Dewlap: A loose or distensible flap of skin on the throat.

Diurnal: Active during the day.

Divergent evolution: Related species or members of the same species that develop different habits or characteristics due to variation in habitat.

Dorsal: Pertaining to the back or top.

Femoral pores: Openings on the underside of the thighs in certain lizards.

Fossorial: Adapted for a subterranean existence.

Gravid: Pregnant.

Gular: Pertaining to the throat.

Hemipenes: Paired copulatory organs of male lizards.

Herbivorous: Eating strictly plant material.

Keeled scale: A scale with a raised ridge running down the middle.

Lateral: Pertaining to the sides.

Nocturnal: Active at night.

Nuchal: Pertaining to the neck.

Omnivorous: Eating both plant and animal material.

Plates: Large, flat, bony scales.

Posterior: Pertaining to the rear end.

Prehensile: Ability to cling or grasp independent of claws. The tails of chameleons are prehensile and act as a fifth "hand" for added stability in trees.

Racial variant: Subspecies.

Sexual dimorphism: Outward physical variation between the sexes of particular species.

Subspecies: Variation within a particular species as to color, geographical range, or habits.

Terrestrial: Living primarily on the land.

Toe pads: Special organs on the toes of geckos and a few other lizards. They contain minute hair-like structures that catch any irregularity in the surface the animal is standing on and keep it from slipping. This allows geckos to walk up walls and even cling to a pane of glass.

Thermoregulation: Maintenance of optimum body temperature by cold-blooded animals via alternately basking and cooling off in the shade.

Venom: Poisonous substance produced in special glands in the lower jaw of gila monsters and beaded lizards.

Ventral: Pertaining to the belly or bottom.

Xenosaurus grandis, a Mexican xenosaur (Xenosauridae). Photo by Dr. S. A. Minton.

Xantusia vigilis, the desert night lizard (Xantusiidae). Photo by F. J. Dodd, Jr.

Right: *Heloderma horridum*, the Mexican beaded lizard (Helodermatidae). **Below:** *Heloderma suspectum*, the gila monster (Helodermatidae).

Bibliography

Boulenger, G.A. 1885. *Catalogue of the Lizards in the British Museum.* British Museum (Natural History), London. (Reprinted)

Breen, J.F. 1974. *Encyclopedia of Reptiles and Amphibians.* T.F.H. Publ.

Carr, A. 1963. *The Reptiles.* Time-Life Nature Library.

Cochran, D. and C. Goin. 1970. *New Field Book of Reptiles and Amphibians.* G.P. Putnam's Sons.

Cogger, H. 1967. *Australian Reptiles in Color.* East-West Center Press.

—————. 1975. *Reptiles and Amphibians of Australia.* Reed.

Conant, R. 1975. *Field Guide to the Reptiles and Amphibians of the Eastern and Central United States.* Houghton-Mifflin. (Revised ed.)

Copeia. Quarterly journal of the American Society of Ichthyologists and Herpetologist.

Davey, K. 1971. *Australian Lizards.* Periwinkle Books.

De Rooij, N. 1915. *Reptiles of the Indo-Australian Archipelago, Vol. I.* Leiden. (Reprinted)

Ditmars, R.L. 1933. *Reptiles of the World.* McMillan. (Many reprintings)

FitzSimons, V.F.M. 1948. *The Lizards of South Africa.* Transvaal Museum.

Gans, C. 1975. *Reptiles of the World.* Bantam Books.

Grzimek, B. (ed). 1971. *Grzimek's Animal Life Encyclopedia, Vol. 6, Reptiles.* VanNostrand-Reinhold.

Herpetologica. Quarterly journal of the Herpetologists' League.

Hvass, H. 1958. *Reptiles and Amphibians of the World.* Methuen & Co.

Journal of Herpetology. Quarterly journal of the Society for the Study of Amphibians and Reptiles.

Leviton, A. 1972. *Reptiles and Amphibians of North America.* Doubleday & Co.

Minton, S. and M. Minton. 1973. *Giant Reptiles.* Charles Scribner's Sons.

Roberts, M.F. 1977. *All About Chameleons and Anoles.* T.F.H. Publ.

———————— and M.D. Roberts. 1976. *All About Iguanas.* T.F.H. Publ.

Rose, W. 1962. *Reptiles and Amphibians of Southern Africa.* Maskew-Miller.

Schmidt, K. and R.F. Inger. 1957. *Living Reptiles of the World.* Doubleday & Co.

Smith, M.A. 1935. *Fauna of British India. Reptilia and Amphibia. Vol. II. Sauria.* London. (Reprinted)

Sprackland, R., Jr. 1977. *All About Lizards.* T.F.H. Publ.

Stebbins, R. 1966. *Field Guide to the Reptiles and Amphibians of the Western United States.* Houghton-Mifflin.

Taylor, E. 1963. *The Lizards of Thailand.* Univ. Kansas.

Index of Common Names

Page numbers set in parentheses refer to illustrations.

Top: *Anelytropsis papillosus* (Anelytropsidae). Photo by Dr. S. A. Minton. **Bottom:** *Bipes biporus,* a Mexican amphisbaenid. Photo by K. Lucas, Steinhart Aquarium.

Index of Scientific Names

Page numbers set in parentheses refer to illustrations.

LIZARDS IN CAPTIVITY
PS-769